"Phil preaches what he practices, and he's giving away his secrets to help you become the best version of you. If you want to do yourself a favor, read this book, take notes, and make some changes. You'll be glad you did."
– Michael Gutenplan, Entertainer

"Phillip is an expert of self-reflection and an authority on effective communication in the workplace. *All the Reasons I Hate My 28-Year-Old Boss* is a fun and entertaining read; just be prepared to check your ego at the door!"
– Ben Ferguson, SVP Shamrock Consulting Group

"Phillip's vulnerability and authenticity shine like a bright light on important topics of our time. While addressing serious issues of Millennial entitlement, egoism, and nepotism, he successfully brings humor, fun, and ease to personal growth."
– Kimberly Spencer, CEO + High Performance Coach, CrownYourself.com

"Phillip Andrew Barbb finds his passion in serving people. He has a heart for helping others to discover their purpose, while building strategies to help them achieve their goals so they can thrive."
– Josh Ochs, Founder of SmartSocial.com

"Contagiously positive and energetic, Phillip educates on ageism while entertaining at the same time. You're sure to enjoy this casual, interesting read that has lots of great tips you can begin implementing immediately."
– Mario Spagnuolo, Business Owner, Soprano's Catering, Catering 2 You, Mannino's Bakery

"Coming from the entertainment industry, Phillip is no stranger to navigating intense work environments. Even with the pressures of Hollywood, he maintains a grateful, can-do attitude, and learns from every situation. In this book, we finally learn what his secret has been all along!"
– Richard Courtney, Television Executive Producer and Showrunner

"Phillip is a dynamic storyteller and a deeply compassionate human being. In this book, he dishes up humor, authenticity, and wisdom, while addressing the touchy topic of ageism in the workplace. Well done!"
– Nicole Jansen, Founder of Discover The Edge and Leaders Of Transformation

"Phillip is an endearing man of action who truly walks the walk. This book is filled with wisdom and helpful ideas to make your work life a more positive one."
– Evan Money, Happily Married, #1 Best-selling Author, Global Entrepreneur

"Energetic and passionate about helping people, Phillip has built a successful career from the ground up, and educates others based on his own life experiences. He is what we, at Underdog Empowerment, call 'A Real M-F-er!'"
– Zachary Babcock, Creator of Underdog Empowerment, Top Rated Entrepreneur Podcast

"Phillip's energy and enthusiasm drew us together as friends and business associates. Reading his book is much like our personal interactions: you are entertained in having spent time with him and walk away feeling richer for the experience. His energy and insights shine through in this powerful book."
– Michael Beals, Trusts and Estates Practice Group Chair, Howard and Howard Attorneys

"Phillip is a man who's dedicated to faith, family, and community. His journey to live out these values in the workplace is a testament to his unique ability to change the world for those around him."
– Chris Phelps, Automotive Account Director

"Phillip is a determined, charismatic, and caring individual who routinely gives of himself to those around him. He truly treasures the development of self for the empowerment of others."
– JaMarr John Johnson, Marine and former Naval Officer turned Speaker and Entrepremedian

"There's no magic pill when it comes to Self-Help books; you have to do the work. Written in his raw, yet lighthearted point of view, Phillip humbly and lovingly serves up the challenge to face the issues of ageism head on."
– Warren Lentz, Director of Creator Partnerships,
Fullscreen Media

"With his positive attitude, confidence, and boyish charm, Phillip's energy is infectious!"
– Brendon Blincoe, former Head of Casting, Iconic Casting

"In *'All the Reasons,'* Phillip inspires, motivates, and entertains, all in one sweep! Through his wisdom, you will gain valuable guidance on how to thrive in traditional and non-traditional work environments. This book will not only help your career, it will help your life!"
– Aalia Lanius Award-winning Novelist &
Founder of Unsugarcoated Media

"For as long as I've known Phil, he has always striven to be the best possible version of himself. I can't think of a person more qualified to write a book on how to overcome ageism in the workplace, and I look forward to seeing others gain valuable insights to help better themselves as a result Phil's book."
– Sebastian Atwater, Director of Operations, A.I. Technology

"Phillip's advice in this book will help you engage more powerfully with your boss, your colleagues, and with everyone in your life!"
– Virginia O'Brian, Member of The Board of Trustees,
Hugh O'Brian Youth Leadership (HOBY)

"I highly recommend this book if you're looking for a way to get motivated and inspired in a fun way."
– Vali Barbulescu, Award-Winning House DJ, TV Host, and Photographer

"Struggling with time management? Creating a healthy work-life balance can be a challenge. Phillip Andrew Barbb is a master at helping you live an inspired, stress-free life."
– Kris Wolfe, Author of *10 Ways to Win a Girl's Heart*, Founder of GoodGuySwag.com

"Phillip has an ability to connect and identify with people that is rare and authentic. With a humble approach and witty sense of humor, he teaches foundational personal development principles through the use of his own life experiences. This book is a must-read for anyone looking to better themselves!"
– Marc Saltzman, Co-Founder and COO, Crispy Chicken Social Media

"Phil is one of the most inspirational people I know. His consistent, positive energy is contagious, and he has an innate ability to relate to others in ways that instill confidence and strengthen their human capital. Phil brings a unique perspective to personal improvement, and he conveys it in a way that's as fun and authentic as he is."
– Tyler Zaccheo, Advertising Sales Executive

"In the time that I've known Phillip Andrew, he has proven himself to be incredibly trustworthy, hard-working, and honest. His positive mindset and boundless drive are both admirable and unmatched. Anyone seeking a pathway to empowerment should consider reading this book!"
– Andrew Langsam, Entrepreneur

"Phillip Barbb's intentional focus and clarity, genius mind, and genuine humility are something to marvel. What a phenomenal talent. He has an uncanny ability to articulate just what we are all thinking. I look forward to everything he creates."
– Kristine Kuhlman, COO, Trusum Visions

"I can say with complete conviction that Phillip is truly making the world a better place. Phillip lives the quote 'To lead is to serve.' He is someone that you can rely on for sound advice and won't hesitate to tell you exactly what you need to hear even when the feedback is tough to digest. The world needs more humans like Phillip."
– James Peterson, Senior Advertising Partner, Microsoft

"As a business owner, I have struggled with the fear of failure and letting myself and others down. Phillip's advice has helped me flip the switch through implementing positive affirmations and visualization techniques. Phillip helped me get out of my funk so I could make my slam dunk."
– James Ellis, Business Owner, JamesEllisFit

"I met Phillip when he was a senior in high school. As a young man, he showed compassion and an ability to take on new challenges, and now as a mature man and author, he is using those abilities to help others."
– Timothy J. Montemayor, Business Owner, TJ Monte Productions

ALL THE REASONS I HATE MY 28-YEAR-OLD BOSS

ALL THE REASONS I HATE MY 28-YEAR-OLD BOSS

How to fight back against ageism and survive a youth-focused workplace

PHILLIP ANDREW BARBB
2x Emmy®-nominated TV Producer

All the Reasons I Hate My 28-Year-Old BOSS

Published in the United States of America
Trusum Visions Publishing, LLC

ISBN: 978-0-578-58952-7

DEDICATION

As a first-time author, I experienced many challenges as I was righting this book...you know, like finding the right person to proofread it and make sure I was using 'writing' instead of 'righting.'

Pretty early on, it was apparent I was in way over my head, but due to the support of friends and family,
as well as my incredible editor and now friend
Chris Drabenstott, you hold this body of work in
your hands. And that is pretty damn cool.

I dedicate this book to my supportive and loving family:

Christopher Barbb – My fantastic father and my hero since the day I was born. No matter how many times I stumble and fall, you are always there to pick me up, dust me off, and show me unconditional love.

Andrea Barbb – My incredible stepmother who has supported me through all the monumental highs and devastating rock-bottom lows, and you never once saw me as 'not your problem.' Your heart for others encourages me to be strong and supportive; and having you in my life has been, and continues to be, a powerful blessing.

CarolAnn Barbb – You are a fantastic sister and my biggest cheerleader. Your friendship means the world to me, and if I can be a tenth of the brother to you that you are a sister to
me, I can feel like an accomplished 'lil brotherrrrrr.'
(Not a typo)

I would be nothing close to the man I am today if not for you three.

Margaret P. Barbb – While you have been gone for over 15 years, I still feel extremely close to you, Mom. Having you watch over my shoulder and guide me on this journey of life has been a motivating and encouraging power in my life. *Always loved. Never forgotten.*

Since ***All the Reasons I Hate My 28-Year-Old Boss*** is a book about navigating the workplace, I'd like to recognize several individuals who have impacted me in powerful and positive ways in both my professional and personal life.

A special thank you to:

Eli Holzman
CEO, *Industrial Media*

Kevin Bartel
CEO, *Best Production Company*

Damon D'Amore
Founder & CEO, *Legacy Mentor*

Jacquie Jordan
CEO, *TVGuestpert*

Andrew Martz
Financial Advisor, *WIS Advisors*

Rob Stone
Radio Host, *99.5 WYCD Detroit's Country*

Charles Kreisa
Executive Producer

Anthony Powell
Founding Pastor, *Redeemed Life Church*

Travis Lutz
Executive Coach, *The Good Life Program*

Daniel Weingarten

Stand-up Comedian & Writer, *@DWComedy*

Steven Garcia

Executive Producer, Director, Vice President of Current Programming & Development, *B17 Entertainment + Thumb Candy Media*

TABLE OF CONTENTS

Should you read this book?

All the Reasons I Hate My 28-Year-Old Boss
is an entertaining, comedic, and motivational business and self-help book for

- Business Professionals
- Artists
- Creatives
- Mothers
- Fathers
- Cats
- Dogs, etc.

Anyone who has ever worked with a co-worker or for a boss with a problematic personality,

YES, this book is for you.

The overarching theme of this book is AGEISM, so it is essential to take a look at where it comes from and how we have been socialized to accept it, and why it kicks us in the ass as we get older.

So, here is my agreement with you:

After finishing this book, you will feel empowered, enlightened, have a new peace within yourself, thriving in your current position, and will be on your way to building a stronger relationship with your younger boss. (Or, you'll be ready to fearlessly hand over a letter of resignation to the little piss-ant drowning in his dad's oversized suit.) Maybe you will be inspired to go out there and become your own boss! To hell with the 28-year-old prodigies; become your own prodigy. Or perhaps you will learn a new way to approach dealing with that little diaper-filler. Either way, get ready to examine *All the Reasons I Hate My 28-Year-Old Boss*, and let's overcome the injustice of ageism together so we can get on with living our best lives.

WHO'S WITH ME?

FOREWORD

In my 30-plus years as a leading international authority in behavioral conditioning, personal development, and organizational culture, I've had the privilege to mentor and coach corporate executives, industry-leading companies, and even a handful of those entitled Millennials. (I even raised a few of them, myself.) Thanks to the tech-savviness and more up-to-date skillsets of Millennials, those who are considered Baby Boomers and Gen Xers are having to compete for management roles like never before. So, how do you deal with the 28-year-old intern who just became your 28-year-old boss?

Phillip Barbb is a master of his craft in helping people become more strategic and effective communicators; and in this massively entertaining book, he humbly and humorously draws on his own personal experiences in life and the workplace to deliver solid, principle-based teaching on how to navigate and overcome ageism. The quality and integrity of his personal character, his genuine enthusiasm to bring value to the world, and his fun-filled Millennial/Baby Boomer banter...well, that's just the icing on the cake.

Phillip boldly introduces the proverbial elephant in the room, illuminating the everyday challenges of stereotyping, prejudice, and discrimination that inevitably come with working with people across multiple generations; and he uses effective coaching methods that lead to a more positive, win-win outcome for everyone. Skipping over the legalities, Barbb goes straight for the jugular with his in-your-face approach to modifying the mindset and re-thinking common, ageist perspectives.

As the saying goes, "Age ain't nothin' but a number" ...until it threatens your livelihood. Whether you've been passed over for a promotion or unceremoniously urged to retire, *All the Reasons I Hate My 28-Year-Old Boss* addresses the common frustrations, annoyances, and mental hang-ups of being a member of the American workforce, and it presents actionable steps and sensible solutions for handling ageism in today's youth-driven workplace.

So, grab a cup of coffee, pull up your rocking chair (or your hoverboard), and enjoy this ageism intervention. Whether you're a Baby Boomer, Gen Xer, Millennial, or Gen Zer, not only will this book have you laughing yourself silly, it will challenge you to explore your deepest beliefs through honest self-assessment exercises, which will empower and equip you to thrive and succeed in the workplace, no matter how old (or young) your boss is.

Rod E. Hairston
CEO, Trusum Visions,
International Best-Selling Author,
Global Keynote Speaker

Guess what, your boss is an asshole!

Just kidding, they're probably not. At least I hope not. They could actually be quite great if you got to know them; and a positive working relationship with them may very well be the next monumental turning point in your career and your life. (It might even put more money in your family's travel fund, too!)

Something about this book jumped out at you.

- Maybe you've been struggling to get motivated at work or notice that the typical day-to-day of the workplace has turned you into a "Walking Dead" zombie.
- Perhaps you are switching career paths and now find yourself starting over.
- You may be very successful in your career, but due to the economy, now find yourself working in a new environment where all your co-workers seem to care more about their social media feed than the company's bottom line.

Hell, your boss probably cares more about eating avocado toast than almost anything else. Here's the good news: I am here to help and offer some new perspective and guidance! (By the way, if you don't know what avocado toast is, we better get to work!)

I want to thank you for picking up this book! I hope you will have as much fun reading it as I did writing it.

Ageism in the workplace, otherwise known as age bias or age discrimination, is becoming increasingly more prevalent in today's business world. While many employers would like to think their companies don't engage in this type of discrimination, statistical data and the growing number of age-related discrimination claims prove otherwise.

The Equal Employment Opportunity Commission (EEOC) records over 21,000 age discrimination claims each year. Additionally, a research pole discovered that 64% of older workers say they have either seen or personally experienced ageism in the workplace.

The resulting consequences to employers, workers, and job seekers are damaging and far-reaching. It is therefore imperative that a change in mindset and a proactive, targeted approach is utilized when it comes to effectively addressing and tackling the current issues surrounding ageism in the workplace.

Is the Problem Real or Is Ageism Just Another Trendy Buzzword?

We've all likely encountered stories from within our business networks when scanning the professional social media websites or while talking with family members and friends who talk about the topic of age discrimination in the workplace. All too common examples include job seekers age 40 and over being told that they are overqualified, will cost too much to employ, and that they are a cultural mismatch for the organization. Or worse yet, they find themselves being blatantly ignored when applying for jobs for which they are fully qualified. When it comes to employed older workers, examples include being passed over for promotions in favor of younger, less-experienced workers, being replaced by less costly Millennials, finding their jobs suddenly and abruptly eliminated, or being unceremoniously forced into early retirement. Unfortunately, the ugly issue of ageism is occurring more frequently than employers would like to admit.

When reviewing the median age of some of America's top companies, it is natural that it would cause some workers' blood pressure to begin to rise:

MEDIAN AGES OF EMPLOYEES BY COMPANY

Company Name	Median Age	Company Name	Median Age
AOL	27	Facebook	28
LinkedIn	29	Salesforce	29
Google	30	Apple	31
Amazon	31	eBay	32
Adobe	33	Microsoft	33
Dell	35	IBM	38
Oracle	39		

The reality of ageism and its consequences make this problem far more significant than just another trendy buzzword.

Sounds pretty scary, huh?
Just wait...there's more.

Today's Multigenerational Workforce and Factors for Consideration

It is estimated that Millennials will account for approximately 35% of the global workforce by 2020, and they are spread across all levels of companies, including managerial roles.

The growing percentage of Millennials in the workforce is not the only factor that is making matters interesting. In today's unique time in history, we have a workforce demographic that is comprised of "Baby Boomer", "Gen X", "Gen Y" (aka: Millennials), and "Gen Z."

DEMOGRAPHIC	BIRTH RANGE
Baby Boomer	Born: 1946 - 1964
Gen X	Born: 1965 - 1980
Gen Y I Millennial	Born: 1981 - 1996
Gen Z	Born: 1997 - 2012

Employers can easily find themselves faced with the interesting challenge of having to effectively manage not only their workforce but also job seekers that span across these four different demographic groups. The days of workers routinely retiring by age 55 seem to be long gone, with the current age for full retirement now being 66-67 and climbing. For varying financial reasons, including caring for elderly parents or rebuilding retirement accounts that took a hit during the recession, some individuals expect to work beyond their late 60s. This means that employers will need to plan for how they can best accommodate a workforce with employees in their 20s, 30s, 40s, 50s, 60s, and possibly beyond. Employers will also want to consider that 23% of the workforce is comprised of those who are 55 years of age and older. This is far too large of a demographic to dismiss as no longer relevant in the workplace, particularly as this group is healthier, living longer, and more educated than previous generations.

The stage has been set.

This book started at around 250 pages, and then I realized,

'I don't want to read all this s, and I'm the one who wrote it!'***

Luckily, after I spent a week sitting in the corner complaining and crying in a fantastic 'pity party of one,' I received some great advice: "You don't need a lot of content, you just need GREAT content." So, I scaled it down, chose only the best lessons and examples, and now you hold these 170 pages in your pretty little fingertips.

This book is designed to be simple to read, easy to digest, and something you can finish quicker than a bad Netflix binging session.

Also, with a title like *All the Reasons I Hate My 28-Year-Old Boss,* the last thing you want is to be holding this paperback when your BOSS walks by.

So, if you're reading this at work, be sure to place it face down and use it as a drink coaster. (No need to unnecessarily tip anyone off that you're learning about their Millennial ways, #Incognito.)

Now, while the advice and examples in this book are helpful for people of all ages — yes even you, Millennial Dan — it will probably hit home the most for people between 35-62 years old. Sorry, Dan.

The idea that age somehow is
a magic pill of
success, wisdom, honor, and respect
begins when we're pretty young.

At five or six years old, we entered kindergarten and began to believe that the older kids knew more information and were further along than we were. Hell, every fifth grader knows that the seventh grader is an expert and has life totally figured out, right?

That's just common sense.

As we continued to move through adolescence and had more needs and wants, we were told that there are some things we can't have until we are older:

You want to drive a car
but you aren't allowed to because you have to wait until you're older.

You can't see that movie yet
because you aren't old enough.

You can't stay out late
because you're too young.

At many times, age felt like some mythical prison sentence that we could never escape. When will I be an 'acceptable' age to do the things I wanna do?

Time and time again, it seemed as if we were being presented with things we wanted to do, only to have them kept at arm's length by someone older telling us, "You aren't old enough."

But then, things started to happen.
At 16, you got your license to drive.
At 18, "Hello, strip clubs!" (Don't judge me.)
At 21, you are finally allowed to drink alcohol.
#Adulting

Now you're older and starting out on your career path. Before you know it, you're steadily moving up the ranks, you can just see that future corner office — hell, you might even make partner! You can feel the six-figure salary coming.

It is finally your time to get the keys to the palace.

You waited, obeyed, and followed the rules.

You climbed the corporate ladder and made sure not to drink too much at the company holiday party. You did everything right!

It's now time for all of the other 'promises' to come true. You are smarter, wiser, and more distinguished. Your salt-n-pepper hair is really starting to work in your favor. You're not old, you're seasoned.

Then it all comes to a screeching halt when some young, 28-year-old punk decides that all that doesn't apply to him, and he somehow just became your boss.

What...The...Hell...Just... Happened?

Talk about feeling like someone
just cut in front of you in line!

Maybe you switched over to a new, fancy startup where the CEO/Founder could give a rat's ass about your 20-year career. All they know is they're running the show. Maybe you got stung by that nasty little thing called nepotism with your boss' frat boy son who just graduated from university; so, naturally, he is ready to run the division!

"It's not fair," you say. "I followed the rules.
I did what I was told. I played the game.
How come this little shit gets a pass?"

Can you feel the anger brewing?

Can you feel the molten lava of disrespect bubbling through your body?

I know I can. I can also feel a lot of other things, too. I mean, not to kick you while you're down, but to hell with it —it's the whole point of this book!

It isn't just anger and disrespect that are inside of us. It is also:

Entitlement
Fear of Success
Fear of Failure
Lack of Empathy

...oh yea, and let's not forget that big one:
EGO.

"What the hell, Phillip?! I thought you were cool! I thought this was going to be a fun book that makes fun of the Millennials?"

Sorry, my friend. I'm in the business of us all getting better, having a new outlook on the phenomenal opportunities we have every day; and that means we have to face the truth. While I do not deny the very real existence of ageism or want to diminish its injustice*, the truth is, it is a larger issue that will take time and effort from a lot of people to help reverse. For your sake, I want to focus on the aspects of ageism you have control over.

*Know your rights. Information regarding the Age Discrimination in Employment Act of 1967 can be found on the U.S. Equal Employment Opportunity Commission website: www.EEOC.gov.

**Here's the deal:
no one has the power to
make you feel worthless, useless,
or washed up unless you allow them to.**

I don't want that for you, and I certainly don't accept that for myself. I want you to thrive in your everyday life. I want you to experience a renewed purpose. The beautiful thing about feeling sad, angry, lost, and out of control is that with some discipline, understanding, humility, and effort, you can regain control of yourself despite being faced with ageism in your workplace.

*We do not need our situation or circumstance
to magically change.
We have everything we need to be the
happy, fulfilled, energetic, and amazing people
we have always wanted to be.*

"ALL ABOARD THE SELF-AWARENESS TRAIN!"

REASON #1

THOSE DAMN MILLENNIALS ARE SO ENTITLED

***"Millennial this, Millennial that.
I'm sick of everyone catering
to these damn kids.
Participation trophy, my ass!"***

Let's get right into it. I don't like to avoid that entitled elephant in the room...those DAMN MILLENNIALS!

It's funny how often we hear the term Millennials, and it typically comes with a negative connotation. We look at Millennials as "the new problem;" however, the term has actually been around since the late '80s. Authors William Strauss and Neil Howe are generally given credit for first using the term to describe children born after 1982, although the specific birth year ranges are largely debated. Many people are beginning to see the problems with having such a wide age range associated with this generation, to the point that a new term has been coined for the Millennials born before 1990 as:

"Old-lennials."

As much as I hate to make such gross generalizations, for the purpose of this book, it is necessary to get into the stereotypes of the exotic species known as *"The Millennial."*

Now, using your best National Geographic documentary narrator voice, let's have some fun by reading the following paragraph aloud (or if your Millennial boss is close by, reading it in your head is okay, too):

The Millennial, wearing its Beats headphones and Kanye West (pronounced "Yee-zee") shoes *loves* to complain. They think he is too old, she is too young, they only eat non-gluten, non-dairy, non-GMO, non-calorie foods — pretty much, anything that begins with "non." They want a promotion yesterday, need to be told constantly that they are doing a good job — wait...did I say a *good* job? I meant great, excellent, perfect, out-of-this-world, spectacular, never-to-be-duplicated by another human again job. She is a princess who always gets her way because she just plain flat-out deserves it. He is Peter Pan — he never wants to grow up. What's the point? They have no respect, they are too soft, and what the hell is the deal with these oversized shirts and skinny jeans?

Okay, are we done yet?

Let's take a deeper look at this "everyone gets a trophy" generation.

In fairness, the Millennials didn't create the world in which they grew up. They didn't have a meeting after tee ball practice to decide that they all deserved that trophy — no, that little gem of an idea came from their parents. They didn't ask for their "helicopter parents" to hover around continually to pick them up and brush them off every time they hit hard times or failed. The parents of Millennials were the ones who thought it made more sense to blame teachers and coaches rather than reinforcing the importance of hard work, resilience, and discipline. Bravo, Millennial moms and dads.

Then you have another side of parenting for the Millennials. Many children grew up in households with parents who viewed their child's accomplishments as proof of *their* success as a parent.

The constant demands of excellence and perfection created a lot of anxiety, frustration, and insecurity for a generation that is now seeing considerable numbers in eating disorders, substance abuse issues, and sexual addictions.

In her book, *The Price of Privilege*, Dr. Madeline Levine, Ph.D. wrote:

"While being involved in after-school activities was good for most children, parental criticism about their performance in these activities was damaging. Holding high standards for our children is not the problem but humiliating and disparaging them when they fail to meet expectations is."

Yes, I am asking you for your compassion and grace.

While there is definitely a difference in the way generations were taught to deal with failure, mistakes, hardship, and how to develop resilience, we must cut the Millennials a bit of a break.

It isn't useful to focus on the problem; so, let's focus on the solution.

We will talk about some of those solutions a little later, but first and foremost,

Be the Example. Be the Light.

Showing others the right way to behave isn't first through your words, rather through your actions. In other words, **"Don't talk about it. Be about it."**

Now, as a quick note to my Millennial friends who are reading this and think I am throwing you under the bus, let's take a look the ancient Greek philosopher Socrates (469-399 B.C.) for a moment. He isn't a Baby Boomer, so you don't have to hate him.

Socrates: "Whenever someone slanders you, you must look at it as if it is just. If it is just, make the change. If not, ignore it."

Thanks, So-Crates. *#BillAndTed'sExcellentAdventures*

Instead of getting all butt-hurt every time you get labeled a Millennial,

stop and check yourself.

Really look at what you are doing — your behavior, your actions, your mentality.

Are you being entitled?
Are you being selfish?
Are you being lazy?

It's not your fault how you were raised, but as an adult, you do have the responsibility — or as I prefer to say, "the ability to respond" — to change your actions.

#Gandhi #BeTheChange

REASON #2

THEY'RE TOO YOUNG TO BE MY BOSS

*"F*** This Dude."*

*"F*** This Dude (or Dudette)."*

Now, I know that might seem a bit harsh. Like, "Whoa, that came a bit out of left field, Phillip!" But I have a confession to make. I've actually said that before!

One of the primary motivations for writing this book is because I realized

I was 100% completely and insanely OBSESSED with age.

I always wanted to know where I stacked up in comparison with other people in my age bracket. Even though I know that thousands of factors contribute to who we become in life, my competitive nature — actually, let's call it what it is, **MY EGO** — was out of control and wanted to be validated with 'I was the best person in the world. I'm SPECIAL.'

Did I mention I was voted Class Perfectionist my senior year of High School? ***Yeah, I'm that guy!***

I would Google everything from:

How much money should I have saved by age 42?
What % of people are making six-figures by age 30?
How many sexual partners do people have by age 35?

(A lil' age-obsessive?
Yup, I'm not proud of it but give me a break...

I'm only human.)

The truth is, I began writing this book, and then something absolutely magical happened. I was feeling powerful and smart and like I was going to save the world with this book; **and then I started a new television job in entertainment.**

I began as a Field Producer on a music documentary series for Netflix called "Westside," and two weeks into my job,

IT HAPPENED.

We had begun principal photography on the project and were in the middle of shooting the first episode. Everyone was getting along great and the team was very strong. I was in a conversation with my boss about our backgrounds, where we were from, TV shows we had produced...and then I asked him the million-dollar question: ***How old are you?***

And guess how old my new boss was? Yup, you got it!
The first thing that popped into my head immediately after he said, "I'm 28" was,

"F THIS DUDE."***

I knew better than that.
I had no idea what experience he had.
I didn't know what his background was.
I didn't know anything about him at all.

I needed to check my attitude, my anger, and my inflated ego IMMEDIATELY!

I was allowing my own AGE-OBSESSED thoughts to get the best of me, and it was stealing my peace of mind.

I felt angry that he was the boss and I wasn't. I felt disrespected that he got hired instead of me. I felt entitled and thought, 'Who the hell is he to tell me what to do and how to do this job?'

**I was pissed. The best part?
This was all AFTER I had already started writing the book!**

I had to get real with myself and ask, "How is my boss being 28 any different than if he had said he was 48? Why would I immediately give him more respect if he was older?"

Sure, I might have said, "Damn man, you look great for 48," but it wouldn't have proven anything about his ACTUAL ability to be successful at his job.

I realized I needed to treat him like a man who was simply hired to do a job. I can't second-guess his decisions because of my own stupid prejudice. I can't give him an attitude because I have entitlement sweeping over my heart.

I need to do the job that I was hired to do and let him do the job he was hired to do.

The competitor in me says, **"I will be wayyyyy better at my job than he is at his. I will crush him. I will prove that his title should have been my title."**

Some people work better being hypercompetitive but that is not the best attitude for everyone. If you told me you planned on using that as motivation, I might advise against it. For me, I know it's not how I best serve other people.

But hell, I said I was a perfectionist, not perfect.

I eventually told my 28-year-old boss about this book, so he knew it wasn't all about him. (Thanks, Ian.)

Because it isn't about him; it is all about ME and how I respond.

The issues in this book AREN'T about your boss or co-workers or mothers or fathers or husbands or wives — they are about YOU.

Your Attitude
Your Approach
Your Entitlement
Your Fears
Your Perspectives

We are going to do some serious soul-searching and rewiring before you get to the back cover.

Keep reading if you're ready for some serious transformation.

REASON #3

THEY JUST STARTED. I'VE BEEN DOING THIS FOR YEARS

"I've forgotten more information than my boss has ever learned."

I get it. You are a stud.
Look at you and all of your success.
Everyone has always looked up to you. They all followed your lead.

They may have even asked you for fashion advice. You're so amazing. **Nice pants.**

You may have awards, keynotes speeches, and medals with your name on them. You very well might have accomplished more than your current boss.

The little kid, the piss ant, the little diaper-filler...*who are they to tell you what to do?*

Can you hear the EGO ALARM going off?
Can you smell the arrogance?

One simple explanation is, you are allowing your successes of the past to justify being arrogant in the present. However, this is deeper than superficial arrogance. What you're really experiencing is the Fear of Failure we all encounter and battle in some way or another.

Despite all of your success, sometimes the future can still feel extraordinarily uncertain; and to step back up to the plate means putting everything on the line again — and that can be scary.

Sports teams know that they cannot rely on last year's success. I bet every Super Bowl championship team would like to be able to relax and enjoy the victory for a little while longer before getting back onto the practice field. However, they know they have 31 other teams all determined to steal their championship trophy, and they need to be prepared. Or as we hear so often, "You are only as good as your last [fill in the blank]."

It is rumored that Shaquille O'Neal would take last year's trophies off his mantel when the new season began. He didn't want to hang his hat on any old awards. He was always looking forward.

In order for you to be the best teammate possible, you have to be ready to suit back up, take risks, and be willing to face the possibility of failure.
Executive Coach Steve Chandler says,

> *"Focusing excessively on the past is just a way out of the present. It's a bailout, it's a flight. It's an escape."*

You are living in the past.
You are focusing on your reputation, and you know what? **You are afraid.**

That's right, I said it.

You're afraid that you will fail.
You are trying to hang on your old successes, but the truth is, when you do not live in the now, you are cheating yourself out of life. By mentally hanging onto your past accomplishments, you are letting your ego prevent you from trying new things.

Do not be held prisoner today with the fear of duplicating yesterday's success.

You should be so lucky to fail at something today. With failure comes the opportunity to grow, and the truth is, we are pushing our limits and have the chance to develop our character into a purpose-driven one that is resilient to the struggles of today.

Life isn't about chasing success and avoiding failure. Trying to avoid failure only prevents us from taking the necessary risks toward progress.

You should want to CHASE FAILURE.

Your goal should be to find a little bit of failure every single day. If you uncover enough failure in your life, then you will eventually discover lasting and fulfilling success. You already know this to be true: your career is filled with examples of you overcoming setbacks and pushing through toward accomplishment.

However, somewhere along your journey, you forget how comfortable you should be with failure. "If this kid sees me fail, he might not look up to me. He might think I'm just an old man who's not worthy."

You are worried about your reputation instead of taking ownership of your character.

- A person of character knows they will fail many times if they are genuinely pursuing excellence.
- A person of character isn't concerned with the opinions of others because they know their own virtues and value.
- A person of character is not intimidated by another person; they invite critics, as there has never been a great man or woman in history that hasn't endured a little criticism.

  (Millennials, feel free to replace 'critic' with 'hater' if it feels better.)
- Maybe you've had lots of success in the past and now you feel stuck; or perhaps you are still waiting for your breakthrough.

What can you do?

Two things:

First – Clarify your goals

Second – Do an integrity scan

Let's start with clarifying your goals.

It has been said that *"CLARITY IS POWER."*

I wish I could say I came up with this, but I didn't. A much smarter person than I said it first, but I'm rolling with it now.

It's not enough to say, "I want to be successful" or "I want to help people" or "I want to be a good mother or father." In order to work toward a goal and a way of life, you must first define — with specificity and exactness — what it is you want out of life. A big reason why you may not have it defined is that, on a subconscious level (or conscious level if you have great self-awareness), you are fearful that if you truly define what you want, then you risk knowing you didn't achieve it.

It's the fear-based mindset that tells you:
"You can't drop the game-winning touchdown
if you never step onto the field."

While this 'playing it safe' thinking can be quite common for many of us, we all have more to offer the world than sitting on the sidelines. Have the courage to give some legitimate thought to what you want out of your career and life and be as specific as you can be. Get clarity on your goals.

What advancement are you looking to achieve?

When you define your hopes, dreams, and goals with exactness and clarity, it gives you the power to create the game plan to achieve them. It provides you with the end game to move toward. It tells you what the light at the end of the tunnel will look like.

Clarity helps us fight through the overwhelming feeling of uncertainty and gives us a real understanding of what the next steps need to be.

Of course, things may change along the way, so you re-evaluate and redesign your approach as you continue down the path. You don't even need to know each and every step right this second, but you have to set your aim with real, quantifiable, and easy-to-comprehend goals.

And remember, you can only reach the light at the end of the tunnel if you are MOVING through the tunnel.

Do the work.

Get off of the bench and get into the game. Learn to love the process. Define your goals with extreme precision and clarity because

CLARITY IS POWER.

Have you noticed how we began this chapter talking about your boss, and now we are solely focused on you? Yes, get used to it...it is going to happen a lot.

The fact is, every person in the world is outside of your realm of control.

You can influence people (just as I hope this book will impact you if it makes you better and happier), but the choice is still yours.

You can't change your boss (or husband, wife, the barista at Starbucks...) but you can take responsibility for yourself to become happier, more joyful, and to have a greater peace of mind.

The second thing that you can do is take an **Integrity Scan.**

You are either:

Inside of integrity
or
Outside of integrity.

The dictionary defines integrity as,
"The state of being whole or undivided."

When I talk about being "inside of integrity," I am talking about being **whole and undivided.**

When I talk about being 'outside of integrity,' it means your character is experiencing dissonance and is in a state of **incompleteness.**

I want you to read this list of values, one at a time, considering what each one means to you:

AUTHENTICITY	RESPONSIBILITY	BOLDNESS	WISDOM
CREATIVITY	FAITHFULNESS	HARD WORKING	KINDNESS
UNDERSTANDING	LOVINGNESS	LOYAL	OPTIMISM
RESPECTFULNESS	HAPPINESS	SERVICE	RUTHLESSNESS
PEACEFULNESS	FRIENDLINESS	ADVENTURE	TRUST
SPIRITUALITY	COMPASSION	TRUTHFULNESS	KNOWLEDGE
HONESTY	ENCOURAGEMENT	DEDICATION	ACCEPTANCE
CARING	GRATITUDE	DISCIPLINE	INSPIRATION

Now, choose the top five values that are the most important to you — the ones that you would hope your friends, family, and colleagues would describe you as. If you have a value that isn't on the list above, feel free to use your own.

WRITE THEM DOWN HERE:

____________________ ____________________

____________________ ____________________

____

I don't pick them for you.
Your boss doesn't pick them.
Your mother doesn't pick them.
The choice is yours!

*These values must be **important** to you, deep down to your core.*

Now, here comes the challenge:

It isn't enough to simply pick your five values and then call it a day. After all, Enron chose the values of "Respect, Integrity, Communication, and Excellence," and I'm sure you remember how things turned out with that scandal! Values only work if you embody them and practice them.

Look at the first value you selected. Over the past week, *how many times did you behave in the opposite way of that value?*

For instance, if you selected HONESTY but you lied to your boss about why the report wasn't finished, that is in direct conflict with your own integrity. ***#OutsideOfIntegrity***
If you selected FRIENDLINESS, yet you were rude to the barista at Starbucks this morning because they misspelled your name on your Venti cup, you are operating outside of integrity.
If you selected DISCIPLINE, yet you didn't go to the gym this week when you said you would, you are outside of integrity.
(Random fitness tip: set out your workout clothes and shoes the night before so they are ready in the morning.)

As mentioned before, when you are outside of integrity, you are **incomplete.**

You are experiencing dissonance in your character and in your core beliefs. You are going against what and how you want to be. It's easy to see how that can bring anger, shame, frustration, angst, and disappointment.

I don't want you to beat yourself up. That's not the point.

I do want you to be happy, fulfilled, and excited about the person that you are becoming. And the best way to do that is by STEPPING INTO YOUR INTEGRITY.

With integrity comes responsibility, or as I mentioned before, your **ability to respond.**

If being honest is truly important to you, then doing the opposite will leave you feeling incomplete. You can respond by being honest. *All the time.*

Act as if everything you do and say is on camera and broadcast to the world. It sounds scary at first but trust me, it is freeing.

Congratulations! You have achieved CLARITY with five core values that are important to you, and you now have the ability to respond by exhibiting those values in all areas of life so you can be happier and more fulfilled.
I recommend looking at the five values you selected and see how often in the last week you were inside or outside of integrity with those values.

Some call this an inventory.
We will call it a scan.
This is your integrity scan.

Let's get this out of the way: THERE IS NO PERFECT.

Everyone has their bad days. Everyone has their moments where they slip up. We are not saints. That's ok. But you can use this INTEGRITY SCAN to keep tabs on how you are doing. It gives you a better understanding if you are behaving a way that's in alignment with your integrity.
Additional Tip: Take your integrity scan to the next level and incorporate your Five Key Values into a Mission Statement for your life.

REASON #4

SHE'S SO DAMN "BUSY" YET FINISHES NOTHING

"My boss has no time management skills. She's always late and always distracted. She claims to be SO busy, but she never gets anything accomplished."

Newsflash: Looking busy and getting shit done is not the same thing.

Many people in today's society are obsessed with multitasking and "being busy." I am sure you can think of a person or two who seem to confuse talking about getting shit done with actually doing it.

"How you been Mike?"

"Man...busy. Super busy. Good... but busy. Like...kerrrazy busy."

"With what?"

"I mean....uhhh....well...you know. Just crushing it. Hustling and grinding, dude."
#OnTheGrind

This is a fictional conversation. I just made it up. But I've heard similar chats plenty of times...and frankly, I've been on both sides of it, myself.

#Dont Judge My Rise And Grind Monday Motivation Wednesday Wisdom Get Shit Done Hustle

Another thing about a lot of Millennials is that they *have* been busy...since they were four. Think about it: many kids grew up being ushered around from school to soccer practice to choir practice, while doing homework in the back seat of the car, while heading to coding class. Oh yeah, don't forget about

Spanish and Chinese language lessons on Tuesday, and Yoga for Tots on Sunday mornings.

To make matters worse, parents will compare their children's jam-packed schedules with the jam-packed schedules of other kids. Quite often they judge their own parenting skills harshly and are constantly concerned about whether or not they are setting their kids up for a successful future. The trap is that parents become too focused on extracurricular activities and miss out on important quality time with their child. There's something to be said for life "back in the day," when being busy meant riding bikes together as a family.

When we spread ourselves too thin, we are setting ourselves up for disaster.

In their defense, many Millennials have never experienced any other way to be. This creates a trap of striving to accomplish ten tasks in a half-ass sort of way, rather than getting three things completed in their entirety and done well. We all claim to be "so busy;" however,

we need to be intentional about what is making us "so busy."

Being busy doesn't automatically mean that you are being effective.

"How are you?"
"Oh man, so busy."
"Really? What have you been busy with?"
"I mean, you know. This and that. Life. Just busy."

Sure, we have a lot 'going on' in our world today; and like it or not, a lot of what is 'going on' is merely a distraction (aka: a whole lotta nothin').

LOTS AND LOTS OF DISTRACTIONS.

How effective you are will be determined by how well you can sift through the meaningless and mundane "busyness" that is plaguing our society and by putting in hard work that is disciplined and intentional toward well-defined goals.

Executive Coach Steve Chandler says,

"Busyness is laziness. It is lazy to be busy. It's lazy for me to occupy myself with all these small tasks when I know deep down that none of them will produce wealth. This 'busywork' is an enemy to my financial success."

Remember, even the ANTS are busy. You have to ask yourself, "What is keeping me so damn busy?"

Are you actually working toward real goals or do you spend much of your time being distracted?

Are you going through the motions of life and calling it busy in an attempt to make yourself feel better?

Are you busy so you can hopefully avoid someone asking a favor of you?

Are you saying you're busy because it makes you feel productive and worthy of respect?

Take ownership of your actions, be deliberate with your time, invest in yourself and your personal growth.

Take a long, hard look at how you spend your time, the things you are "busy" with, and ACCURATELY EVALUATE what things can be shifted, changed, or better yet, eliminated, in order to make time for the things that will bring you more excitement and fulfillment in life.

A person sitting in a rocking chair may be busy rocking that chair, but are they going anywhere?

Make sure you are putting the "right amount of busy" into the right activities, or else you will have incomplete projects all over the freakin' place.

In sales, it is commonly said that 80% of your revenue comes from your top 20% of clients.

It's not about having a thousand clients that you spend a couple of emails/calls on; but it is absolutely essential to have those 25 that you dedicate a significant amount of time to.

If you are going to dig a well, you drill ONE 100-foot deep hole, not 100 one-foot holes.

This concept might take your boss some time to understand. Sometimes, people get distracted in the day-to-day and can't see the forest through the trees.

Don't get caught up satisfying your boss' BUSYWORK if you know it isn't going to produce results.

Have the courage to describe this concept to your team. Educate them and stress the importance of seeing tasks through efficiently, and to completion.

It is imperative to set boundaries in the workplace.

Timothy Ferris offers a ton of examples for this in his book *The 4-Hour Workweek*. I am sure you read it. We all did.

Remember that jam-packed schedule we discussed of the Millennials? It should provide some understanding as to why your young boss thinks they need to be busy all the time, even if that busyness is merely rocking in a chair.

The busywork can *feel* right, it looks like motion, but we know we aren't going anywhere.

It is your job to have the strength to use your energy for the things that are going to produce real results — not just satisfy a culture that's based on helping "helicopter parents" have more bragging rights at PTA meetings.

REASON #5

HE HAS SO MUCH TO LEARN

"This little bastard doesn't know sh** about life."

Remember back to high school, and how we thought the younger kids had no clue and that they were 'in over their heads?'

We knew we were further along in Math, Science, English, skipping class, parallel parking, and we were even better kissers.

Those silly little freshmen had so much to learn.

This way of thinking is a common
trap for students, and sadly,
many of us have never grown out of it.

We carried that mentality into our adult lives, and we now assume that anyone younger than us

has no idea in hell what they are doing.

We remember ourselves at that age and think,

'Hell, I was an idiot.
Why would they be any different?'

While it's easy for people to operate under the assumption that everyone comes from the same path, it is an absolute lie.

We make assumptions about everything from politics to economic status to the choice of what cars people drive.

We judge.
We stereotype.
We're human.

We often make the mental error of thinking that everyone comes from the same (or similar) background as our own. We project our life experiences onto them, assuming they had the same upbringing.

We all are unique people. And in the same way that your boss doesn't know all of the ins and outs of your life, *you surely don't know the ins and outs of theirs.*

For example, I will share a little story about myself.

I am super BRO-y.

If you can picture a guy wearing a lime green tank-top with a backwards hat, aviator sunglasses, driving around in a Jeep Wrangler with a cheesy custom license plate...welp, that's me.

Don't believe me? Just check out the license plate.

"Easy Bro."

You can't make that shit up.

I'm a cartoon character.
If Johnny Bravo met Southern California, that would be me.

It would be easy to put me in a box and imagine me hitting on girls at the beach while ripping shots of tequila and crushing Coors Light cans on my head, but you would have me all wrong.

The truth is, I have been sober from alcohol since January, 2008.

I began drinking alcohol at 11 years old, and from the very start, I was using alcohol to cope with the anxieties and insecurities of adolescence.

While I did an excellent job of keeping any signs of the problem under the radar, the drinking continued through middle and high school.

When I was 14, my mother was diagnosed with cancer, and after a year-long battle, she passed away a week before my 16th birthday.

I was sad and broken, angry and destroyed.

Despite going through this experience, I stayed true to my reputation of being an overachiever. It was an obsession. I continued to make the honor roll, be a captain in varsity sports, and participate in student government.

I didn't want anyone to know how much pain I was in, and that is when the drinking started to take over.

After a couple years, I had not-so-proudly accomplished:

- *A drinking and driving car crash at the age of 18*
- *Two minor in-possession-of-alcohol arrests at 19 and 20*
- *Too many fights to count – I won a couple but* ***lost*** *them all*
- *An emergency room visit where I received seven staples in the back of my head*
- *...and...wrapped it all up with a DUI arrest only three blocks from my childhood home*

I was crushing life, all by the mature age of 22.

(Now, *that's* what you call being 'busy.')

Often times, when people learn of my past hurts and hang-ups about drinking and they hear of my time abstaining from alcohol, they are very supportive and speak with praise. They're downright proud of me.

While I appreciate the support, I always remind them that the length of time I've been sober isn't the critical part.

I am proud of the man I have become in that decade. I am proud of the work I put in to becoming a better man and to better serve other people.

The shame, the guilt, the embarrassment, the tears, the honesty, the vulnerability, the transparency, the healing...

The self-awareness I developed is what I am most proud of and what I value the most.

The hard truth is, I have met many people who've gone over 25 years without having a drink that are also

sad, angry, miserable, and flat out assholes.

The length of time away from a bottle is not always correlated to a person's level of wisdom, fulfillment, and serenity.

I even had a significant amount of time during my journey where I was miserable, frustrated, and cynical, and it was all because I wasn't working a proper program. I was feeling entitled, I failed to evaluate my behaviors in an honest way, and I was petrified to make the changes I knew in my heart I needed to make.

The reason I tell you this story from my own experience is to showcase that while having over ten years without alcohol is indeed a milestone, it is not a guarantee that a person will have developed the character that is to be honored and respected.

Time is not the only factor when we look at someone's abilities. Wisdom doesn't necessarily come with age; ***wisdom comes from putting in the work to become wise.***

This is just as true when it comes to our careers. Having 15 years invested in a given profession isn't a guarantee that that person is the best one for the job.

I once heard it put this way:
"There is having ten years of experience,
and then there is have one year of
experience, ten times."

There's nothing wrong with respecting someone's longevity and dedication, but that is just one aspect of validation.

The Five Variables of Training

I once read of an outstanding plan for determining the effectiveness of a training regimen. It was written by a Navy Seal who discussed the following five variables of training:

1) Frequency
2) Intensity
3) Duration
4) Recovery
5) Reflection

If you only look at one or two of these factors, then you only see a small piece of the puzzle. The same is true when you attempt to predict a person's level of influence and projected success without having the full picture.

If you only look at *duration*, you consider *how long* someone has been in a job position or an industry.

Frequency describes *how often* they have been in a career.

Intensity is *how hard* they are striving in that career.

Recovery will show how well they allow the hard work to settle in and change them for the better.

Reflection is how self-aware, willing to learn, and how open they are to readjusting their approach.

To give someone credit because they have been working in the same career for an extended amount of time is to ignore **80%** of the equation.

You must look at the full picture.

One way to truly understand the totality of a person is to see them as more than an employee or coworker or boss and view them as a companion. Approach them as a person that you are on a team with, working toward a goal that is bigger than both of you.

Instead of saying, "This little bastard has no idea about anything," take the time to get to know their full story.

You have no idea the path that they have had to travel to get to where they are. When you take the time to genuinely understand someone and who they are, you can massively shift the relationship.

It's easy to stereotype people and think you have them all figured out based on one characteristic.

Don't be that person.

Be the person that asks questions.
Be curious.
Be authentic.
Be a great companion.
Be a great human.
Be the best you.

REASON #6

HE'S A MICROMANAGING LITTLE PAMPER-PANTS

"My boss is clueless — such a little diaper-filler. He has no idea what he is talking about yet tries to teach me things I learned back in Accounting 101."

This also goes for Selling 101, Pipefitting 101, Marketing 101, Advertising 101, Cigar Rolling 101... you get the idea.

No one likes to be micromanaged. It's annoying, it makes you feel like you aren't trusted, and it is about as close to the opposite of occupational freedom as you can get. And the fact that it is coming from someone younger than you makes it that much more infuriating. After all, the babysitter doesn't take orders from the kids they are babysitting, right?

There are two main reasons for micromanagement:

1) The micromanager is nervous, insecure, and has control issues.
2) The person being micromanaged cannot be trusted. Now, since that person in this scenario is you, and you were smart enough to buy this book, we will eliminate this reason because I am sure you are killin' it.

(However, if you indeed cannot be trusted by your boss, get your shit together already!)

Having a boss of any age with control issues can be a challenge. But here is the fascinating thing about control:

"Every single person in the world is outside of YOUR control."

If your boss is a micromanager, you have to deal with it. It may never change; and while it is a pain in the ass, it is still outside of your personal control. Accepting this is a powerful tool.

So, what if acceptance of your micromanaging boss isn't leaving you satisfied and you're still looking for some good, solid advice on how to deal with this pesky Underoos-wearing kid?

OK, here we go...

Try saying something along the lines of "Hey, I noticed that you asked me a couple times about the report that is due on Friday. I know it is important, and I want you to know that I feel confident in completing it on time, and I've got it covered. You don't need to worry about it — it's in safe hands with me. I completely welcome you checking in on me if it will put you at ease, but I know you have a lot on your plate, and this is something I can handle. You can trust me."

Boom!

In using this kind of approach, you are making them feel better, showing that you can be trusted and that you are the one wearing the big boy or big girl pants...and, you did it without being a condescending ass. See how that works? It's always better to make an insecure person feel better instead of fueling their insecurity, especially when that person has the power to fire you.

Side note: Always remember that TONE IS IMPORTANT.

We've all been on the wrong end of a misunderstood text message and experienced the fallout that follows when TONE is misinterpreted. Hell, it's why we have to include conversation cues like "lol", "haha," or your favorite expressive emojis so people know how to interpret our writing.

No doubt about it, tone is pivotal.

So, make sure you are coming from a place of genuine care and service. There is a huge difference between Winnie the Pooh saying, "Don't worry, you can trust me" and Scarface saying, "I got this...say hello to my little friend!" My recommendation: choose Pooh.

Many of us are often misunderstood. We have issues using the wrong tone or fail to come off as genuine and authentic. Here is something to keep in mind before you approach your boss:

SERVING VS. PLEASING.

Remind yourself to come from a place of service.

People-pleasing is small.
People-pleasing contains an element of desperation.
People-pleasing can be codependency in disguise.

In *The Prosperous Coach*, Litvin and Chandler write,

> "Pleasing others is the real reason why people don't succeed. And in the end, pleasing others doesn't win any respect from them either."

When someone is focused on being a people-pleaser, they can come off as needy or a kiss-ass or just flat out annoying.

Instead of wondering 'What should I say that will make them happy and like me?' ask yourself,

"How can I serve them?"

Serving people is a benefit to everyone. We serve other people out of strength, power, and confidence. When we serve people, we are lifting everyone up.

If you can master serving vs. people-pleasing with your boss, it will help when it comes to your husband, wife, kids, at the parent-teacher conference, or when you get pulled over for texting those fun, little emojis while driving.

REASON #7

MY BOSS IS AN EGOTISTICAL PRICK

***"My boss is an egomaniac.
I was never like that
when I was their age."***

Oh, like you weren't.

As much as we like to draw distinctions between the generations, the truth is, your first boss probably said the same thing about you when you were 28. Hell, perhaps even worse.

You weren't perfect.
Think about all the mistakes you made when you were your boss' age.

I remember reading about a young man who stood under 5'8" tall and weighed less than 150 pounds. He had a great sense of humor, was extremely reckless, and allowed his ego to get him into more trouble than he could manage.

His name was William McCarty, and he began his criminal history by stealing clothes from a laundry.

He then progressed to stealing horses and earned himself the nickname of "Bad Boy of the West." Since he loved to witness the chaos his dirty deeds created, Williams's ego often brought him back to the scene of the crime. He believed he was "untouchable," and that very belief led to his ultimate demise.

After being arrested for the murder of a local sheriff, he escaped from the Lincoln County Courthouse. Instead of keeping a low profile, William's ego brought him out of hiding, and authorities quickly discovered him. After a wild shootout, the young man lay bleeding on the ground covered in dirt and gun smoke.

And who was William McCarty?

If you ever saw the movies "Young Guns" or "Bill and Ted's Excellent Adventure," you might have already guessed it:

Billy the Kid. We have all heard the legends.

You think Billy the Kid's ego was because he was a Millennial?

HELL NO.

This "Kid's" ego was because he was a young and immature man, and that is as true in 1880 as it will be true in 2020 or in 2180.

#YoungAndReckless

Stop blaming Millennials for being young. Have some compassion. It takes time to develop the wisdom that can only come from years and years of experience.

Quick Reminder:

Ego is often just a front for extreme insecurity.

Your boss is nervous that they will screw up. Remember that little thing called fear of failure?

Here is another fantastic lesson from the history books about ego:

→ STOP TRYING TO OUTSHINE YOUR BOSS.

This little gem comes to us from Spanish author Balthasar Gracian's *The Art of Worldly Wisdom* written in 1647, which states:

"Avoid outshining your boss...They may tolerate being helped, but not surpassed. Therefore, let advice you give them appear more a jog to their memory than a beacon to what they couldn't find. The stars teach us lessons, because, though her children are bright, they are never so forward as to outshine the sun."

Obviously, *'All the Reasons'* deals with how today's economy and work environment is changing and creating new, uncharted age role-reversals, but let's take age out of the equation for two seconds.

Most people hate being embarrassed.
I would go so far as to say that NO ONE LIKES BEING EMBARRASSED. (Other than your crazy Uncle Lou, who wears a bra on his head when he gets drunk at Christmas dinner. I don't think he cares much about embarrassment.)

No one wants to be told they are wrong, to feel stupid or belittled. So, why would you do that to anyone, especially your boss, regardless of their age?

I am not suggesting that you be a '*YES MAN*' and be silent when you see a better way of accomplishing tasks in the workplace.

I am saying BE SMART and look at the interpretation, not just the intent.

There are ways to get your point across without outshining, embarrassing, belittling, or exposing your boss' mistake or failure.

When you genuinely want to HELP, remember the People-pleasing vs. Serving idea that I mentioned in the last chapter.

Take the approach of SERVING someone and the business as a whole.

By *removing your EGO, everyone can move forward and grow.*

I often ask myself,

"Am I trying to PLEASE people right now, or am I trying to SERVE them?"

When you answer this question honestly, after some deep introspection, you will be led to the right approach. I'm sure of it. If your words or actions are harmful to your boss' self-esteem, more than likely your **EGO** is way out of whack, regardless of how great your thoughts or ideas are.

Check your ego, and don't try to outshine your boss.

My boss thinks she knows everything. She thinks she is God's gift to the IT department! I'm going to send her an email virus.

First off, don't do that.

Second, as mentioned earlier in the 'Quick Reminder,' your boss is a human. A person.

Just like you, they are filled with fears and insecurities.

Regardless of what your feelings are telling you, your boss wants to do well. They don't want to make mistakes. They don't want to get fired.

No one likes being on unemployment, except for your crazy Uncle Lou — remember him?
While your boss may be exuding arrogance, they could quite possibly be terrified.
Be the one that supports them.

Think Service.
And don't **assume** you know more than they do.
Do I need to write it again?
Check your ego.

I'll write it a couple more times.

Check your ego.

Check your ego.

Check your ego.

Hey, you. Yea, *YOU!*

I hope you are having a good time so far. You may have even learned a thing or two.

I greatly appreciate you taking the time to read this book. It means a lot to me, and I hope you are enjoying it.

The sad truth is that most people only read about 15% of a book; then life happens, and they close the cover. The good news is, if you're on this page, you've already made it past 15%! Kudos!

Now, I want to ask you for a favor:

Please go to **Amazon.com** and give this book a review.

It helps to get the word out there, and I truly believe that learning more about ageism will lead to a better workplace and better world.

Thanks in advance

for your feedback.

Now, let's get on with it...

REASON #8

HE OVERSIMPLIFIES EVERYTHING

*"My boss oversimplifies everything.
He wants everything ASAP,
and it's just not that simple."*

Several years ago, I was working at a UK-based TV production company on a development project for the Lifetime network. After several days of editing a casting presentation, my Executive Producer asked me if I could fix a particular part of the video. He wanted a better sound bite to help make the casting reel make more sense.

I was a little annoyed since I had been working on it for days, and I wanted nothing more than to check it off of my To Do List.

In an attempt to get him off my back, I claimed that I knew the footage like the back of my hand, and there was no way that what he wanted was even possible. I mean, why mess with perfection?!
I told him very firmly and confidently that the sound bite he was looking for simply did not exist.

My Executive Producer paused for a second, smiled, and said something to me that I'll never forget:
"Phillip, think about YES before you say NO."

These words have stuck with me (ok, haunted me) throughout my career.

Since I realized he wasn't going to let this task slide, I adjusted my attitude from one of laziness into a spirit of defiant ego. I was determined to search the video for hours just to prove to him that what he wanted didn't exist. I would show him and

prove him wrong. Period, end of story. He had laid down the challenge and my ego eagerly accepted it.
I prepared myself for the sound bite hunt. I knew there would be hours of scrolling through footage.

I was fueled by the desire to be right and was imagining my glory as it would ultimately be determined that I was so smart and capable — no one should ever question me ever again.

I began the mission.

Only 35 seconds into my search, I found the sound bite we needed. I adjusted the video, and the new edit was completed and fixed in less than two minutes.

Two minutes!

Let me point out that I had spent a solid ten minutes arguing with him that what he wanted wasn't possible. Needless to say, I was as proud as I was embarrassed.

I was letting my ego get in the way of doing the job I was hired to do.

The truth is, I was lazy and behaving like a child.
I didn't want to work on the video any longer.
I was bored with it, and I just wanted it finished.
I was acting entitled, stuck in my own
("right") way of doing things,
and I didn't want to do it another way.

Have you ever made a mountain out of a molehill before? ***(That was a trick question...I already know you have. We all have.)***

Okay, that's enough about me. Let's talk about you. You have probably been in your industry a long time. You know the ins and outs. You know that you can't just run out and make the changes your boss wants in an instant.

"This isn't how this industry works."

Or at least that is what you are telling yourself.

Have you ever said something couldn't be done, only to see it get accomplished with what appeared to be little or no effort? (Ummm...whoops.)

Obviously, I learned this lesson the hard way.

When you catch yourself being resistant to a suggestion that you don't like or understand, or that might create a little more work for you,

think about YES before you say NO.

Ask yourself,

"Is this better for the project? For the team? For the company? Or, for me?"

Remember that you are being paid not because you showed up to work and are entitled to a paycheck; you are being employed to perform tasks, fulfill a role, and produce results.

As for the oversimplification of assignments in the workplace from your underage boss, let's understand the mindset here. Our modern world is fascinated, dedicated, and outright obsessed with convenience and effortless accomplishment.

For anyone under the age of 28, in many areas of life, they experience extreme convenience and simplicity (thanks, technology), where older people **know the struggle.**

Remember spending hours at the library, digging and hunting through books for a research project back in 1996?

Now, it's as quick and easy as a GOOGLE search.

When you want food but don't want to put on a t-shirt and leave your bed, there's GrubHub, Eat24, and UberEats. **#convenience**

If you want a movie, **Boom**! You can download it directly to your smart phone.

If you want new music, with just a couple of clicks, it's playing.

Need to buy a book, a shirt, a blanket, or a lawnmower in two days without putting any pants on? **Thank you, Amazon Prime!**

Everything over the last decade has become damn near instantaneous and a borderline invitation for serial laziness. To Baby Boomers or Gen Xers, this is something that's new; but for young professionals and Millennials, *it is all they have ever known. Ease and convenience is (and has been) their way of life.*

Are you getting this? You can understand how they have been conditioned to think that things are just naturally going to be easy.

They love instant gratification because it's always been there for them.

Understand their outlook and make sure that you aren't over-complicating things.

Are you too set in your OLD ways? (I know, that probably stung a little bit, but you'll be ok.)

Have you been doing it one way for so long that you've forgotten the old saying "There is more than one way to skin a cat?"

Where's your flexibility and adaptability?

Don't be the old dog who's not willing to learn any new tricks. It is a new day. Embrace it.

Sometimes, the adjustments and the corrections really are that simple.

Your attitude is what needs the adjustment.

Quick exercise:
If there are some areas of life that you feel you could use some updates in, list them here.

In what areas do you think you are failing to update/upgrade your thinking?

____

____

____

____

____

A common phrase you want to be cautious of is

"It's easier said than done."

Imagine you are in a sales meeting, and your boss explains new strategies they want to implement for the company. You lean over to your co-worker and half-heartedly mutter, *"Pfff... that's easier said than done."*

Or picture your boss inviting you into their office to discuss ideas on how to boost productivity from the IT department. You're thinking to yourself, *'They talk about opportunities, but I only see challenges.'*

They ask if you think their request is possible, and you reply with, "It's a lot easier said than done, boss."

Well, no shit, Sherlock.

We hear it all the time.

"Easier said than done."

Whether it is doing homework, getting out of bed when the alarm sounds, keeping your kitchen sink clean, talking about living with honor, treating others with love, or working toward your career goals,

practically any and everything in life is 'easier said than done.'

Whenever you hear a suggestion that you think will take more effort than you are currently willing to provide, you say it.

It is such a DEFEATIST way of thinking, isn't it?

In using this phrase, you are instantly giving yourself permission and self-justification as to why it's ok to FAIL. It allows you to accept the mentality of, 'Hell, why even try? It probably won't work anyway.'

The truth is, 99.9% of things are easier said than done. But that doesn't mean you don't do it.

It's actually ridiculously EASY to SAY almost anything. But you know what they say... "Actions speak louder than words."

#NikeJustDoIt

Saying "It's easier said than done" is nothing more than an EXCUSE.

It is a statement that admits you don't want to take the necessary action to achieve the desired result. You are absolving yourself of the responsibility to act by allowing the perceived difficulty of the task or situation to win.

You are playing small.
You are fearful.

Don't allow the fact that something is HARDER to do than say prevent you from actually doing it.

In Brendon Burchard's *Motivation Manifesto*, he points out

"When we are called into ACTION by life, and we fail to act, AT BEST, we are lazy. AT WORST, we are a coward."

We are not meant to be cowards. We are not meant to be afraid. We are called to be greater. We are called to be courageous. We were created to be resilient, strong, bold, and powerful.

Stop holding yourself back by allowing yourself to use the excuse that it is easier said than done. Don't worry about how hard it might be. If you know it is the RIGHT thing to do, then JUST DO IT!

"Don't wish it were easier, wish you were better."
– Jim Rohn

Have the courage to develop a spirit and identity of ACTION.

REASON #9

SHE OVERCOMPLICATES EVERYTHING

"My boss overcomplicates everything. She is always lost, confused, and her indecisiveness is giving me an ulcer!"

In the previous chapter, we addressed ways your boss can tend to oversimplify everything. Now, we are going to explore how they can seem to overcomplicate everything.

SO, WHICH IS IT, PHILLIP!?

Whether you are upset that your boss overcomplicates or oversimplifies, it really doesn't matter.

What matters is how you respond.

While it may seem like your boss is overcomplicating situations for no reason, let's take a deeper look at what may be causing this. They may be afraid of making a wrong decision; or maybe they're so massively indecisive, they struggle in making any decisions at all! Or perhaps, it's just a matter of knowing how to make a move when the pressure is on.

Or, overcomplicating could just be part of their process.

They might like to think about a situation from all different angles, internally create a pros/cons list, and analyze the various possibilities and outcomes in order to make the best decision. You may perceive it as overcomplicating when they see it as being thorough.

Abraham Lincoln famously said, *"Give me six hours to chop down a tree and I will spend the first four sharpening the axe."*

Not everyone is a 'shoot first and ask questions later' kind of decision maker. Allow people to work according to their own process.

Now, you may be saying, "But Phillip, you don't understand. This little bastard kid of a boss is too damn indecisive. If they would just listen to me, everything would be fine. I have the experience and the answers, and they just won't listen. It's driving me nuts!"

Regardless of the fact that you're older than your boss, *you are not their parent.*

They are an adult too, who should be allowed to make up their own mind. It isn't your position to tell them what to do because you're older. Instead, try supporting them through their decision-making process. Instead of offering direct advice (aka: "You should..."),

try on some good ol' curiosity by asking compelling questions.

In Michael Bungay Stanier's book *The Coaching Habit*, he describes the importance of

"Taming the ADVICE MONSTER."

I LOVE THAT. As a personal development coach, taming the advice monster helps me recognize when I am getting a little too preachy or overbearing with my clients, friends, co-workers, the lady in the car next to me, the tank-topped 'bro' on the treadmill near me at the gym, and yes, even my boss.

Ask "Why?"
Then ask "Why?"
And then ask "Why?" again. *

After all, there are tons of different learning styles, and everyone formulates their responses in their own way.

For instance, I used to struggle while shopping for shoes. I needed to see every damn pair of shoes in the mall (sometimes in three malls) before I could feel confident in pulling the trigger on purchasing the perfect pair.

I was terrified
that I would buy a pair of shoes, then
march into a different shoe store and find a
better pair for a better deal. Then I would
resent myself
for being so impulsive.

I need to research;
I need to know all the options.

* *"Why Do Kids Ask Why?" is another blog post @PhillipAndrew.co/Blog*

Then there are others who feel completely overwhelmed with having all those possibilities. They'd rather just get in, get out, and get on with it.

Ever heard of something called **Choice Paralysis?**

> As defined by Wikipedia, choice paralysis is *"the state of over-analyzing (or over-thinking) a situation so that a decision or action is never taken, in effect paralyzing the outcome. A decision can be treated as over-complicated, with too many detailed options, so that a choice is never made, rather than try something and change if a major problem arises."*

As fascinating as choice paralysis is, I'm choosing not to dive into it here.

Bonus Video Material:

A few years ago, I produced on a Science and Psychology show for YouTube Red called "Mind Field" with Michael Stevens of the Vsauce channel. We were nominated for two Daytime Emmys® for *Outstanding Educational or Informational Series.*
(You'll love it.)

In episode 5, "Freedom of Choice," we examined choice paralysis.

Check it out if you are interested in understanding more about how your brain handles choice.

Sometimes we make fast decisions. Sometimes we need to think through every possible option and potential outcome. If every human acted the same way, it would be a pretty dull planet.

It's healthy to allow people to navigate their own processes and accept that you are not in control of others' lives.

Now, I assume you are not an asshole.
(at least not all of the time)

I'm sure the frustration with your boss is coming from a place of wanting to help them out, right? You probably just want to save them from themselves — you just want to help. (#sarcasm Or, maybe not.)

In the addiction recovery world, there is a saying,

"You cannot cheat someone of their bottom."

Rather than being the savior, there are times when you need to sit back and patiently wait while someone goes through their own process. You know how you can hear something a number of times, but it's that *one* time when it's said by the right person at the right moment where it finally hits you over the head as if it's the first time you heard it? That's what I'm talking about. You can't control when someone is *really* gonna get it.

Lifeguards learn this in training:

If someone is drowning, they're usually panicking and violently thrashing their arms around. Lifeguards learn to approach the swimmer from behind to get them out of harm's way. If they don't, they risk being dragged under the water by the victim.

If you don't know how to help someone, you may soon find yourself in over your head. (Pun intended)

Whether your boss (or wife, husband, son, daughter, cousin...) is overcomplicating or oversimplifying a situation,

Ask powerful questions instead of letting that ugly "advice monster" show its face.

The advice monster is more likely to stir up resentments than positive change.

The last thing you want is a boss that is resentful toward you.
Beware the Advice Monster!

REASON #10

IT'S AMATEUR HOUR

"My boss doesn't even know how to tie a damn tie; what a little twerp. What is this... AMATEUR HOUR?"

I wish I could say something brilliant about this.

I wish I had something really witty to write, something extremely insightful.

But I can't. I got nothin'.

Honestly, Amateur Hour is just one of my favorite phrases. I think it's hilarious.

I know it doesn't move the needle forward, but it's fun. And that's a big part of why I'm writing this book — to make all this ageism stuff fun to learn about.

Maybe one day I'll grow up, but for now...

It's Amateur Hour.

REASON #11

THEY SPEND MORE TIME ON SOCIAL MEDIA THAN WORKING

"Twitter this, Instagram that...my boss is obsessed with social media. Who the hell cares about ghost chatting?"

You can't write a book about younger bosses and Millennials without addressing the impact that social media has in the workplace.

I first discovered Facebook in 2004 as a freshman at Michigan State University.

I remember thinking,
*'What the hell is this?
Why would I want this? No thanks.'*

I thought it was a phase.
How wrong I was!

In my mid-20s, I was invited to a summer pool party in the Hollywood Hills for a startup company's launch of what I thought was a silly little app.

*It was the typical Hollywood crowd:
bikinis, six-pack abs, and lots of hair products.*

At the bar, there was a woven basket filled with little plastic pens with the company's logo printed on it. None of my friends had ever heard of the app company, so I asked what the company did.

After someone explained that the app had something to do with a new thing called 'ride-sharing,' I asked,

"Why the hell would you get into a stranger's car? No one is going to want to get a ride from a random person they've never met. This is stupid."

That silly ride-sharing start-up company happened to be LYFT. (I'm sure you've heard of them **and their $15.1 billion valuation back in 2018.**)

I hope that we've all just accepted the fact that social media isn't going anywhere.

It's not a phase.
It's not a Millennial thing.
It's not a high school thing.
And it sure as hell isn't the root of all evil.

It is a human innovation thing, and it is here to stay. (At least throughout the rest of our lifetimes)

So, let's get into the conversation.

Social media allows us to stay connected with friends and relatives around the world, enables us to more easily learn new trends across countless interests, and provides a way for us to do business in a whole new way.

Now, I'd like to address the great plague of social media, otherwise known as

"The Façade."

For many people who spend a lot of time on social media, they are exceptional at displaying a very impressive exterior mask while their real insecurities gain more and more strength beneath the surface.

Social media provides a perfect environment for people to portray an image that just isn't true.

People can abuse social media in a way that leads to feelings of inadequacy, fear of missing out (FOMO), fear of not being as special and unique as other people; and then these negative feelings can lead to overcompensating, which creates a downward spiral where each photo or post fuels the next. I'm not writing anything you haven't heard before, but a little refresher course can't hurt.

I have a lot of conversations with people where they complain about the behavior of others, and then turn around and fall into the same traps themselves.

While social media is a fairly recent invention, this idea of people wearing masks is nothing new. In 1647, Spanish author and philosopher Baltasar Gracian wrote:

"Some people are all front, like houses half-finished for lack of funds, having the entrances of a palace but the contents of a hut."

When it comes to your team or your boss, take the time to see past the façades and the masks. **Don't fall into the trap of seeing a palace when it's really a hut.** See people as more than just an employee, co-worker, or boss. Look for who they really are under the surface.

Talk with your boss and ask genuine questions to learn more about them.

Ask how they are doing.
Get to know them.
Ask them what's been going on in their life.

People don't remember what you say as much as they remember how you make them feel.

Whether your boss is younger or older,
remember that they're still a human.
Be a friend. Listen.

See beyond the Instagram filters and silly Snapchat faces.

Whether you're a Gen Xer or Baby Boomer who has learned to embrace and love posting on Twitter, or someone who couldn't care less what your 28-year-old boss ate at Whole Foods today, social media is not slowing down — it's not going anywhere. And to be honest, it won't be the last world-changing innovation or trend that you are going to experience in your life.

Think about *The Godfather.* No, not your father's best friend George, who makes inappropriate comments at Thanksgiving dinner. I'm talking about the 1972 Francis Ford Coppola classic movie about Don Corleone.

How much did you enjoy that movie?
How iconic is it?
How important to culture is it?

Well guess what? I never saw it.

Now before you get all up in arms about how I 'don't appreciate the classics' or 'don't care about anything that was made before 2000,' I'm going to make you an offer you literally can't refuse.

Check your judgmental and ageist ego, OR ELSE!

The Godfather is an iconic film, and you probably saw it. Another iconic film is the 1948 Alfred Hitchcock classic *Rope,* which you likely didn't see.

And I have another secret to tell you: I have never seen Lord of the Rings. Any of them.

That might not be that big of a deal to you, but I am a TV producer. I should be well-versed in all things entertainment, right?

I also never saw *Harry Potter* or any of the ten or so *Star Wars* films. (Remind me, how many did they make?)

Sorry, George Lucas!

When people in the entertainment industry learn that I've never seen those franchises, they are always baffled, confused, astonished, and sometimes even angry.

I am sure you have your own musical tastes, TV shows, trilogy features, and Netflix documentaries that you think the world would be a better place if everyone would just check them out.

So, why doesn't everyone just listen to you?

Everyone has their own preferences.

If you have picked up on anything this far in the book, it is that we are each unique and interesting people who come from different backgrounds, educations, interests, neighborhoods, etc.

Let it slide.

Instead of ridiculing people for not seeing a particular movie of your generation, or not knowing who Led Zeppelin is, try introducing them to it.

If you think it is a disservice to the world that they never saw *Girls Just Want to Have Fun* with John Cougar Mellencamp and Sarah Jessica Parker, then send them a clip via email, or better yet, step up your game with an interesting meme.

#MemeGameStrong

For all my salespeople out there, you know that better results come when you showcase a benefit to your client rather than ridiculing them for being behind the times. (Unless, of course, you are dealing with a person who's still rocking a Razor flip phone. Then, it's open season — ridicule away.)

Think about how you can serve your boss and your co-workers, and you will always find yourself in a better position to get your way.

Here is another example to *drive* this home. (Here comes the pun...)

People in Los Angeles love to complain about the traffic.

"The damn 101 is a parking lot."
"There are just too many cars...y'all need to go back to Nebraska."

The traffic is so bad that L.A. residents shy away from making plans with people that live on the other side of the 405 freeway. In a city filled with people trying to prove they belong, some think that by hating L.A. traffic, you prove that you are jaded enough to belong. (They don't call it Holly-Weird for nothing.)

Here is the truth: driving in L.A. is something people do every day. There aren't many options for avoiding it.

So why complain about something you *know* you have to do every day?

It makes much more sense to learn how to love the traffic. Embrace the time alone. Enjoy the weather. Cue up a good audiobook and relax.

Complaining about the traffic in Los Angeles is like screaming about having to tie your shoelaces.

Either buy slip-on shoes or quit your crying. I like to use this same approach when it comes to social media.

If you relate to the above stories and social media is driving you up the proverbial wall, *try a social media cleanse.*

I get it, the word cleanse feels so "California," but it's what we do out here. You don't need to delete all the apps forever but give yourself a good month off. You can give everyone a heads up if you want, so they don't wonder if you got kidnapped and tossed into a ditch. Trust me, your friends and family will still be there when you've completed your cleanse. (After all, they are just as obsessed as you are.)

A few years ago, I was right in the middle of a social media cleanse at a time when I was producing a digital series for YouTube Red called "Mind Field." I was driving from the University of California-Irvine back to L.A. with the host of the show, Michael Stevens. As we were in the car chatting about social media, psychology, medical advancements, and whatever else I could think of to try to prove I was smart, I realized that this was a great social media opportunity.

I wanted to post an Instagram photo, a Snapchat story, and a Facebook update. I thought, 'I know I'm on a social media cleanse, but this won't take long; it'll be quick. **Hell, maybe just a little tweet.'**

In my head, it all made perfect sense.

This was my moment to show everyone how cool I was, and that I know famous people, and I work with them, and they drive in my car.

(Even just writing this, I realize how ridiculous that mindset is, but don't act like you can't relate.)

Luckily for me, being on my social media cleanse, I had already deleted the apps from my phone, so they were not easily accessible. (Don't worry, I didn't remove the profiles entirely. I'm not a monster, for God's sake.)

Not having the apps right there, ready to click, I saved myself a lot of embarrassment.

First off, Michael Stevens is a great guy, and he would have had no problem posing for a photo with me; we actually have several together. But it gave me time to sit and ponder a couple of fundamental questions:

- Why do you want to post this photo so badly, Phillip?
- What are you hoping to get out of it?
- Are you trying to *USE* your friend as a way to prove something? If so, what exactly are you trying to prove?
- Why is that important?

Boom!

I went into
in-depth self-analysis,
and it made me
understand
how social media
can have
a hold over us…
especially me.

While self-reflection is always helpful, it also gave me some time to practice self-discipline.

I had committed to a social media cleanse.
I had set a goal. I had made a decision.
If I'd opened that app and posted a photo,
even when I told myself I wouldn't, I would've
been proving my lack of discipline.
Do I risk that? Do I open the app? **No way!**

I chose to enjoy that moment and connect with Michael instead of worrying about "the façade." It allowed me to be present for our road trip from Orange County back up to L.A.

By shifting my focus to real, authentic, genuine human relationship (vs. virtual ones), I was able to stay present in a social environment with another human. I stopped trying to connect with everyone in the digital world and chose to build a more meaningful relationship with someone who was sitting right next to me.

That mindset has helped me focus more time on local people in my area instead of trying to 'live in the cloud.'

Side Note:
If you love science and technology,
please check out
Michael Stevens'
YouTube Channel, Vsauce.

REASON #12

A DIRECT MESSAGE TO MILLENNIALS

"Baby Boomers destroyed America. Walter really needs to retire. This guy still has an AOL email account."

I am sure there are a handful of Millennials out there scheming to get some quality info out of this book to use against their older co-workers.

You bought this thinking it would be like **studying the enemy's playbook.** Oh, you clever little Millennial... trying to get a leg up.

You overachiever, you!

Hey, it totally makes sense. I get it.

After all, it's why (for dating research purposes) I have a subscription to Cosmopolitan Magazine...used to. I mean, I used to.

How else was I going to learn about:

- *"How to Tell if He's Good in Bed"*
- *"Your Breasts Called...: And They're Feeling Neglected. How to Pamper & Pleasure Them"*
- *"My Car Turned Me On!: Hilarious Tales of Accidental Pleasure"*

Yes, all REAL articles from Cosmo Magazine. Swear to God.

Anyway...

I understand you may be a hotshot, a fast riser, a prodigy... **but no one gets far in the long run when you're running it alone.**

Become friends with your older co-workers, colleagues, and subordinates. Why?

Despite their differences with the way you grew up, they still have a lot of knowledge and wisdom for you to soak up. It's true. There are very few things that are substitutes for experience.

You are sitting on an untapped gold mine with some of your more experienced employees.

One of the significant characteristics of a successful leader is

being open to opinions and suggestions that are in direct conflict with your own beliefs.

Here's why it matters: you may learn a thing or two, and your business (and life) will be better for it in the long run.

Being able to accept constructive criticism, even from your employees, is a huge sign of maturity, and it can be extremely helpful in building rapport with your team, as well as achieving greater self-awareness.

Abraham Lincoln used to fill his presidential cabinet with advisors who would question his judgment and challenge him, so that he knew he was viewing all sides of an issue.

And they put him on the $5 bill, so you can trust him.

Famous author and life coach, Tony Robbins, often tells the story of when Barack Obama asked him for coaching.

Tony told the president that he would offer advice but wanted to be upfront about the fact that he did not agree with his political agenda.

People in the room gasped. How could he? Everyone was shocked, offended.

Everyone except for *'No Drama Obama.'*

He understood the importance of having people that can push you and challenge your thinking.

If you want to grow, don't surround yourself with 'Yes Men' and 'Yes Women.'

If you can learn to do the same, you too can be like Abe Lincoln. (And maybe they will put your face on some bitcoin.)

Or at least, maybe your employees
won't call you a jackass behind your back.

REASON #13

HE HAS NO WORK-LIFE BALANCE

"My boss has no friends,
no family,
no hobbies...
all he does is work 24/7
and expects me to do the same.
I have a life, damnit!"

I have worked for bosses who were completely glued to their desks — emails being sent at 3:40 am, pillows and blankets kept in their office "just in case," wearing the same clothes on Monday as they wore on Friday.

Alright, maybe I'm exaggerating just a bit; and when it comes to describing your workaholic boss, more than likely, so are you. Your boss is not an alien or robot that runs on coffee and gets their highest fulfillment from keeping an empty email inbox. Your boss is a human who may be experiencing some difficulty with managing work-life balance, just the same as most other people in the world who struggle to juggle career, health, fitness, entertainment, friendships, relationships, parenting, soccer practice, yoga class, the newest superhero movie, etc.

We hear people talk about Work-Life Balance all the time:

- You need to take more time to enjoy your life.
- You need to make more time for fun.
- You work too hard.
- You don't work hard enough.

Or the ultimate mantra:

"Work hard, play hard."

Perhaps the easiest way to illustrate
this mantra is by imagining
work-life balance
as a **playground SEESAW.**

Why do we tend to express the balance of work vs. life as if they are in direct competition? It's as if there is a silent war happening inside of us stating, "As your work is thriving, your personal life is crumbling."

The work-life balance is viewed by many as a 'zero-sum balance.' This zero-sum philosophy is, *As one end goes up, the other must come down.*

Doesn't that sound depressing?

I SAY, "TO HELL WITH THAT!" That is NOT the truth. That is NOT the way it has to be.

Most of us spend more than 40 hours a week at work. We are cheating ourselves if we choose to see this time as something that's in direct conflict with an enjoyable personal life.

Our careers offer us the ability to enjoy a ton of fun, excitement, and fulfillment if we are willing to change and reshape our mentality toward work.

In Mihaly Csikszentmihalyi's book, *FLOW: The Psychology of Optimal Experience*, the psychologist talks about how we can create our own GAMES inside the workplace that help bring more enjoyment and purpose to our jobs. Csikszentmihalyi states,

> *"Contrary to what we usually believe, moments like these, the best moments in our lives, are not the passive, receptive, relaxing times—although such experiences can also be enjoyable, if we have worked hard to attain them. The best moments usually occur when a person's body or mind is stretched to its limits in a voluntary effort to accomplish something difficult and worthwhile. Optimal experience is thus something that we make happen. For a child, it could be placing with trembling fingers the last block on a tower she has built, higher than any she has built so far; for a swimmer, it could be trying to beat his own record; for a violinist, mastering an intricate musical passage. For each person there are thousands of opportunities, challenges to expand ourselves."*

You have the power to shatter the idea that work and life are competitors, and instead, marry them together and learn to enjoy your work, regardless of how difficult, repetitive, or stressful you've previously chosen to perceive it.

Stop considering your career as an evil necessity of life. Stop seeing it as an annoyance. Regain control over your outlook toward your work.

This is one of the keys of self-mastery.

When you work toward self-mastery and apply what you've learned to your work-life balance, you can enjoy a situation where you no longer have to feel torn between them. You can have your cake and eat it, too.

Now, I can hear you saying, "But Phillip, what about my boss? *They* are the one with no work-life balance."

GIVE THEM A COPY OF THIS BOOK!

HAHA...seriously though,
you can only control yourself.

Your boss' actions and outlooks are outside of your realm of control, just as everyone else's is. If your boss is making unreasonable requests with regard to your work-life balance, then it may be time to set some boundaries and expectations.

Take pride in knowing that I wrote this book for you, not for your boss. Focus on the adjustments you need to make in your own life before you try to change your boss or colleagues.

REASON #14

SHE'S SO IRRESPONSIBLE. SHE REMINDS ME OF...ME!

***"My boss is as irresponsible as my kid.
I don't know what's harder:
getting an answer from her or getting
my kid to clean his room."***

Do you ever feel like different people in your life all seem to be making the same annoying mistakes? Perhaps everyone seems lazy, or pushy, or lacking moral character. Have you ever thought that your boss acts just like your reckless child, or your boss behaves the same as your unorganized husband?

It seems crazy that the people in your life all seem to suffer from the same character flaws, right? It's almost like you are on a prank TV show where everyone teamed up to make your life a little more difficult, just for the fun of it.

WHAT IS WRONG WITH EVERYONE?

If those last paragraphs felt all too real for you, guess what? More than likely, the problem isn't with them, it's with you. (GASP!) Now, before you get all defensive and bent out of shape, I want to share some information with you about a little defense mechanism called psychological projection.

Our good friends over at Wikipedia describe psychological projection as

> *"a defense mechanism in which the human ego defends itself against unconscious impulses or qualities (both positive and negative) by denying their existence in themselves while attributing them to others."*

Psychological projection
is used to protect our precious egos.

By taking an internal conflict you have with yourself or with anyone else and pushing it outward onto a specific person or group of people, you have unconsciously chosen to participate in the mental gymnastics of projection. It allows you to avoid addressing, taking responsibility for, and dealing with your own internal conflict.

Projection gives you a feeling of superiority over others while simultaneously overlooking your own insecurities. It causes you to focus on the negative attributes of others, which can then strain those relationships, and more importantly, keep you from building awareness of your own areas for personal growth.

The projection also prevents you from identifying the underlying feelings that are generating the unconscious conflict. The short-term denial of your internal feelings will do nothing more than allow for the feelings to grow stronger and more difficult to overcome in the long run.

We must make sure we are not
projecting our own personal frustrations
and resentments from
people in our personal lives onto
the people in our professional lives.

"I can never get my husband to do work around the house, so, it's no surprise I can't get my boss to lift a finger in planning the company Christmas party."

I have a secret to tell you:

Your boss is not your spouse.
They are not your child.
And they are not the annoying Uber driver who got lost on the way to the airport.

Leave problems from home at home. Even if your boss does something similar to your husband or wife, they are not the same person.

Oftentimes, psychological projection leads to unfair generalizations.

- Just because one doctor was incorrect in your life does not mean that all doctors are incompetent.
- Just because one woman or man broke your heart, does not mean you'll never experience true love.
- Just because one person your junior was defiant and immature, does not mean they will all treat you with disrespect.

As they say in new relationships,

"Do not punish your new boyfriend or girlfriend for the actions of your ex."
#LeaveYourBaggageAtTheDoor

When looking at your (younger) boss, ask the questions:

How well do they complete their tasks?
How well do they treat people?
How well do they work with others?

It is crucial to treat each person as an individual. Don't fall into the trap of lumping them into a category because it makes you feel better. If you're doing this, you're most likely projecting.

Try the following exercise to help you become more aware of psychological projections that may exist in your life.

Projection Exercise:

Write down some common frustrations you are currently experiencing in your personal life, and then identify ways those frustrations could be playing out in your professional life. Since this goes both ways, try to identify feelings you have in the workplace and how you might be bringing them home and projecting onto people in your personal life.

Then repeat the exercise by looking for areas of life where past experiences may be negatively impacting your current outlook on people, places, and things in your life.

Personal vs. Professional

Personal Conflict	Professional Conflict

Past vs. Current

Past Experiences	*Current Situation*

BONUS:

Now that you are more aware of psychological projection, I want to introduce another fun psychological phenomenon that affects our subconscious minds and the way we perceive others. It's called

The Halo Effect.

The Halo Effect is the tendency for positive impressions of a person, company, brand, or product in *one* area to positively influence one's opinion or feelings in *other* areas.

An example of the Halo Effect might be perceiving someone as being more intelligent, more successful, and more popular if they are attractive and well-dressed.

Anyone who spends more than seven minutes watching television and pays attention to marketing and advertising knows that this cognitive bias is used to influence our behavior, as well as our bank accounts. But in order to navigate the workplace in a fair and equal manner, it is important to understand the Halo Effect, **and its evil twin the "Horn Effect,"** which causes a person to perceive someone else as completely awful, based on a single negative trait. You might assume that someone is incompetent and lazy because they have wrinkles in their shirt. Remember, you are not the iron police.

Understanding the Halo and Horn Effects and their influence on your subconscious feelings toward others prevents you from falling into the trap of treating people differently based on a specific set of (often misleading) characteristics.

REASON #15

DAMN, AM I THE PROBLEM?

***"Holy Crap. Maybe I'm the problem, not my boss.
Damn. I am the one creating all of
this havoc. Damn. Damn, Damn, DAMN!"***

I love to beat myself up mentally.

Okay...that's a damn lie. I hate it! Haha. I wish I wasn't so hard on myself, but I'm working on it.

I'll bet you can be pretty hard on yourself, too.

Think about how many times you've said, "I am my own worst critic."

Why do we do that? There must be some reason, right?

I mean, it doesn't make us feel good; it doesn't serve us.
So, why do it?

I had an epiphany the other day:

It was Veterans Day, so I went to the Los Angeles Memorial Cemetery near the campus of UCLA to pay my respects to fallen soldiers. As I was walking past the gravesites and reading the awards and honors achieved by these men and women, I began to reflect on my own life and replaying specific moments from my childhood. This trip down memory lane led me to ask myself some interesting questions:

- "Why I am so hard on myself?"
- "Why do I beat myself up so much?"
- "Why is it so difficult for me to forgive myself after I've made a mistake?"

After much thinking and walking, the answers came, and it was all quite simple:

I've been doing it for a long time.
I've had a lot of practice with it.
And I've gotten pretty damn good at it!

At some point in childhood, in an effort to seek approval and mask my insecurities with others, I developed the habit, and I never corrected the behavior. *It's that simple.*

It's just a bad habit.
Nothing more. Nothing less.

It's almost silly when you think of it that way, isn't it?

Could it be time to do some course-correction and build some new, more positive habits? **I think so.**

So, here is a speedy, three-step process for the next time you catch yourself beating yourself up:

1) RECOGNIZE

Recognize the fact you are doing it. It's hard to correct a habit that you aren't aware that it exists. Recognize when you are beating yourself up.

2) INTERRUPT

Interrupt the bad habit and replace it with a new, better one. Instead of using the usual negative self-talk, immediately create a new, positive statement that better supports you. Lucky for us, we don't have to be stuck in childish thinking any longer.

3) ENCOURAGE

Encourage someone else. Instead of tearing yourself down, get out of your own head, take a moment, and build someone else up — about anything! Call or text message someone and genuinely encourage them. It'll uplift you more than you know.

It has been said that "All suffering is an obsession with self."

Stop obsessing over yourself and go encourage someone else.

RECOGNIZE the behavior, INTERRUPT the habit and replace it with a better one, and ENCOURAGE someone else.

It is essential to look at your thoughts and behaviors closely to evaluate whether you are creating a life that serves you.

Being able to take a look at yourself, honestly and fearlessly, is another crucial component of self-mastery.

Remember the Integrity Scan from earlier in the book?

It's necessary to practice self-awareness and reflect on how you are living your life. However, it doesn't do you any good to relive your mistakes and beat yourself up about it.

You shouldn't live your life punishing yourself for every moment when you fell short of perfection.

YOU MUST LOVE AND OFFER GRACE TO YOURSELF.

{ Progress Over Perfection }

Is all this advice backed by science?
I don't know.

I'm not a scientist.

This information is backed by my own personal experience and the experience of people I've worked with.

I am much happier
when I love myself and love others
vs.
scolding myself for not being perfect.

RECOGNIZE * INTERRUPT * ENCOURAGE

Bonus Material:

Thank you to my good friend and comedian Daniel Weingarten, who tipped me off to some very important terms and descriptions put together by **Anxiety Canada™:**

"Thinking Traps" to avoid:

Fortune-Telling:	"I know I'll mess up."
Black-and-White Thinking:	"I planned to eat healthy, but I had a piece of cake, so now my diet is a complete failure."
Mind-Reading:	"Other people don't like me."
Labeling:	"I am a loser."
Overgeneralizing:	"I will never be good at giving presentations."
Overestimating Danger:	"If I have to recreate that report, I will die."
Filtering:	"One person left during the presentation so everyone must have hated it."
Catastrophizing:	"I'm going to fail, and then everyone will laugh at me, and there will be a Facebook page created where everyone talks about my failure, and I will never be able to go out in public again."
Should Statements:	"I should never make mistakes, and I should be a millionaire by the time I am 25 years old…or else, I'm a loser."

https://www.anxietycanada.com/sites/default/files/ThinkingTraps.pdf

REASON #16

THAT KID IS CRUSHING LIFE ALREADY...I WISH I COULD START OVER

"This little bastard has his entire life ahead of him... Youth is wasted on the young."

Quick Tip:

Anything that comes out of your mouth that begins with 'young, little, baby-ass, newborn, half-grown, fledgling, unripe, pubescent...'

means that your ageism is holding you back.

Many of us struggle with focusing too much on what we don't have instead of what we do. We have all been sold the idea that

'there is no substitute for time.
You can't get it back.
Once it's gone, it's gone.'

It's easy to reflect on what you haven't done with the time you have been given, and then judge yourself harshly. If you have friends or family who've passed away, it makes your own mortality seem that much more real.

But the key isn't to focus on the years you feel you may have lost. The key is to focus on the years that have yet to come.

Let me let you in on a little secret. When you say,

"These damn kids have their
whole life ahead of them..."

Well, SO DO YOU!

Honestly, *nothing is guaranteed.*
All we have is today.

Billions of people have come and gone in this world who never reached your current age, and while it may be morbid as all hell to think like that, some of these pubescent bosses or co-workers of yours may not make it to the age you are, either.

Car Crashes * Cancer * Suicide * Heart Disease
Homicide * Liver Disease * Stroke * Drug Overdose

According to the Center for Disease Prevention and Control, more than 7,000 people die every day in the United States.

7,000.
Every Day.

Each day is precious and filled to the rim with moments deserving of gratitude. When you focus on living in the now and work on appreciating what you have, you will forget about what you *don't* have.

Don't live five years in the future and ten years in the past.

Be present and excited to live in the current moment.

Whether it's 50 more years, 5 more years, or 5 more days, do not be concerned with the perceived time that other people have left in their lives, but be focused on how to make the most of the time you have left.

One way I do this is to **make a gratitude list.**

<u>Try it for two weeks.</u>

Don't be a stubborn shit.
It'll only take five minutes a day for the next two weeks — you can handle it.
As a matter of fact, you can get started right here, right now!

____

____

____

____

____

____

____

If you're still being a stubborn shit and you left the lines blank, here are some examples to choose from:

- I have a full head of hair.
- I am bald, so I don't have to spend money on hair products.
- My kids didn't turn out to be drug dealers.
- My arms and legs work.
- I have leisure time in my life to sit and read a book about my annoying 28-year-old boss.

- I didn't have to do anything for my heart to beat and my lungs to keep breathing during the night. They just worked.
- The Detroit Lions won the Super Bowl.
    - (Ok, I don't know what year you are reading this in, but I have high hopes — there's nothing wrong with trying to **manifest** it into existence, right? Let it be known, if the Lions win the Super Bowl within the next ten years, you have Phillip Andrew Barbb to thank.)

After you have made your gratitude list, read it back to yourself OUT LOUD. There are powerful things that happen to your soul when you are thankful and show gratitude to the universe. Give it a try!

You have already spent more time reading this book then it will take you to do this exercise over the next 14 days.

Let me know how it goes.

Connect with me on Twitter: @PhillipAndrewLA

Now, you may think I've been a little tough on you and your current way of thinking.

You're not alone; I have been guilty of ageism as well.

It is actually one of the biggest reasons I wrote this book.

I noticed that I was allowing people's ages to affect my own confidence, self-worth, and work ethic.

The truth is, whether you are 65, 55, 45, or 21, comparing yourself with others based on age (and a million other factors) is normal. It's also more detrimental than you probably realize. Comparison leads you to judge those younger than you as immature, inadequate, and incapable. But you don't have to take my word for it, after all:

Theodore Roosevelt famously said,

"Comparison is the thief of joy."

You can trust him. My next examples might not have stellar reputations on par with the 26th president, but it doesn't mean they can't provide solid arguments against ageist thinking.

Let's switch from a politician to sport, as we take a look at the highest payday boxing match in history.

After years of training in MMA, in 2017, 29-year-old **Conor McGregor** made his boxing debut in his match against Floyd Mayweather (then, 40 years old).

McGregor was paid $30 million
to fight Floyd Mayweather.
$30 million!

Conor McGregor earned a net worth of about $85,000,000, and he hadn't even reached his 30th birthday.

What an accomplishment.

McGregor didn't let his age get in the way of him chasing his dream. As a matter of fact, there were some who felt that his younger age even gave him a leg up on Mayweather.

Nevertheless, experience did win.

Mayweather in ten rounds...BOOM! Plus, Mayweather walked away with $100 million from the fight. Not a bad payday for him, either.

To my 40-something friends who are reading this book, take some pride. Hell, a boxer at age 40 has a "health age" of about 75.

Switching gears, for any of my movie buffs out there, the movie *War Dogs* told the story of two young men who managed to trick the US Government into a massive military and weapons contract during the war with Iraq. The story was first reported in Rolling Stones magazine's article: "The Stoner Arms Dealers: How Two American Kids Became Big-Time Weapons Traders," and then it turned into a Hollywood blockbuster.

Business partners David Packouz and
Efraim Diveroli were able to secure a
contract of $300 million for weapons and ammunition.
Packous was 23 and Diveroli was 19.

Now, given the fact that they both ended up going to jail for defrauding the government, I am not saying they should be on a power list of 'Best 25 under 25,' but still...it's pretty impressive for a couple of 'young bucks.'

I took the liberty of compiling a list of some accomplished youngsters and historical figures who experienced tremendous achievements before the age of 30:

YOUNG ACCOMPLISHMENTS

Justin Bieber

It is easy to dismiss 'the Biebs' because he has been in the public eye for so long now, but we forget that Justin was discovered on YouTube before "the YT" was as monumental at finding new talent as it is today. By the age of 15, his first studio album had gone 3x Platinum, selling over five million records worldwide. The Canadian entertainer, born in 1994, now enjoys a net worth somewhere north of $250 million.

Mark Zuckerburg

Zuckerberg was born in 1984, and it is undeniable that he has changed the world with his billion-dollar idea.

At the age of 20, Mark dropped out of Harvard during his sophomore year to found our beloved Facebook, and he is now one of the wealthiest men in the world.

Evan Spiegel

Staying in the world of social media, Spiegel, born in 1990, became the Co-Founder of Snapchat in 2012 at only 22 years old.

Ashley Qualls

While most other middle-schoolers were wondering what the periodic table was, Qualls made her first million at 14 years old. Born in 1990, she created "WhateverLife," which is an online community geared toward Millennials who enjoy Indie Rock, alternative fashion, sex, and relationships.

Now you might be thinking
this has all been made possible by the internet.

Challenge accepted. Keep reading.

But first, just for fun:

Following is a list of successful entrepreneurs and the age they dropped out of college.

Age 19

David Geffen
Founder: *Geffen Records*

Julian Assanger
Founder: *Wikileaks*

Michael Dell
Founder: *Dell*

Bill Gates
Co-Founder: *Microsoft*

Mark Zuckerberg
Founder: *Facebook*

Evan Williams
Co-Founder: *Twitter*

Age 20

Paul Allen
Co-Founder: *Microsoft*

Ralph Lauren
Founder: *Ralph Lauren*

Larry Ellison
Founder: *Oracle*

Jan Koum
Founder: *WhatsApp*

Jack Dorsey
Co-Founder: *Twitter*

Age 21

Dustin Moskovitz
Founder: *Asana, Facebook*

Travis Kalanick
Founder: *Uber*

Larry Page
Founder: *Google*

Steve Jobs
Founder: *Apple*

Side Note:
Richard Branson and Quentin Tarantino both dropped out of high school at 15 years old.

MORE YOUNG ACCOMPLISHMENTS (before the internet)

Alexander the Great
When he was only 16, he founded his first colony, Alexandropis.

Louis Braille

He invented the Braille System at the age of 15.

Joan of Arc

She led the French army over the English at the Battle of Orleans at age 18.

Malala Yousafzai

She won the Nobel Peace Prize at age 17 for her contributions to female education rights.

Jordan Romero

When most kids are climbing trees at 13 years old, Romero managed to climb Mt. Everest. Two years later, he became the youngest climber to scale the tallest mountain on every continent called "Seven Summits" by the age of 15.

Doogie Howser

Doogie Howser was a doctor who...wait a minute. That was a TV show. But there was Balamurali Ambati from Southern India, who did become a doctor and started his practice in 1995 at the age of 17. (I think his favorite show was Doogie Howser, but don't quote me.)

* Bonus trivia: Actor Neil Patrick Harris was only 16 when he landed the leading role in ABC's *Doogie Howser, M.D.*

YOUNG ACCOMPLISHMENTS IN MUSIC

Mozart

Wolfgang Amadeus Mozart was dead by age 35. He passed away from a severe miliary fever, but not before composing 103 minuets, 50 symphonies, 25 piano concertos, and receiving the endearing nickname of "Wolfie."

The Infamous '27 Club'

The iconic 27 Club represents musicians who all died at age 27. This "club" includes Jimi Hendrix, Janis Joplin, Jim Morrison, Kurt Cobain, and Amy Winehouse.

If the list were expanded to include celebrities who died before 30, you'd also have

Jean Harlow	James Dean
Heath Ledger	River Phoenix
Buddy Holly	Brandon Lee
Otis Redding	Selena
Tupac Shakur	Biggie Smalls

...and many more.

None of these people ever made it to their 30th birthday yet they all had huge impacts on our history, society, and pop culture.

Now, don't go crying and complaining about how you never accomplished anything. In the same way the US Military "tears you down to build you up," I have put together a list of people who were late-bloomers and accomplished great things later in life, so we can build up your hope and confidence.

LATE-BLOOMER ACCOMPLISHMENTS

Teiichi Igarashi

Teiichi was 100 years old when he climbed to the peak of Mt. Fuji. Now, it wasn't his first time doing it, but hell...if you can't find that impressive, I'm surprised you haven't lit this book on fire yet and buried it in the backyard.

Peter Roget

He was 73 when he invented the Thesaurus in 1805.

Noah Webster

...yeah, the dictionary dude. A year after the Thesaurus hit, he finally completed the American Dictionary at age 66. It had taken him 26 years. Talk about commitment and persistence.

Colonel Harland Sanders

The colonel was 65 years old when he invented 'fingerlickin good' KFC.

Ben Franklin

Good ol' Ben was 70 when he signed the Declaration of Independence.

Dr. Ruth Westheimer

If sex was your thing, then Dr. Ruth Westheimer was your go-to gal. Dr. Ruth was working at Planned Parenthood when she gave a lecture in 1980 that led to a legendary talk show at the age of 52.

Ray Kroc

Ray was a salesman who had big dreams for the McDonald's restaurants. He spoke with the brothers who owned the restaurant, then founded McDonalds' System, Inc. when he was 52. (And waistbands have been growing ever since.)

Ken Keong

Keong is best known as his character, Leslie Chow from *The Hangover trilogy.* He was in his late 30s and still working as a licensed physician when he filmed the movie *Knocked Up* during a vacation week. While not necessarily considered a 'late-bloomer,' making such a huge career change at the age of 38 would terrify most.

Now, I don't know where you fall in comparison with these ages, but hear my plea now:

Stop comparing!

When I got sober back in 2009, it would have been very easy for me to compare myself right out of 12-step recovery meetings since I was young and hadn't personally experienced many of the stories I was hearing at the meetings. However, I was lucky enough to learn two very monumental things:

1) *Relate to people, don't compare yourself to them*
2) *The power of "yet"*

I was going to recovery meetings in Metro-Detroit, and I was often the youngest person in the room by many years... actually, by decades. I could've easily told myself that I didn't belong because I was just too young, and I didn't fit in.

But I discovered how to listen and how to relate, which enabled me to learn a great deal from them.

I heard stories of people who had lost their husbands or wives, had kids that hated them, had been fired or destroyed their own business, all because of alcohol and drug abuse. None of those things had happened to me...YET.

If I had continued on the path I was on, I very well could have found another DUI, or destroyed a marriage, or hurt myself, or worse, someone else.

"Yet" applies to ageism, as well. Instead of looking at your younger boss in comparison, learn how to relate to them on some level. Look for the similarities.

*Remember that **comparing** divides, while **relating** unifies.*

Combine that lesson with the power of "Yet," and you will be well on your way to achieving some peace of mind. You may not be the boss...yet. You may not have even started pursuing your true passion...yet. You may not have paid off your mortgage...yet. All those things can become realities in your future.

Remember that ***clarity is power.*** Have the courage to write down the goals you have and start taking the steps toward them.

This is your life to live.

As Victorian novelist George Eliot wrote:

"It is never too late to be what you might have been."

In this book, I have identified ways to shift your perspective, and I've given you some actual homework and real-world applications to help you take control of your workplace and your life.

This won't be easy.
There will be resistance.
Life has a way of putting obstacles in the way, like:

BILLS, KIDS, TO-DO LISTS, VISITATION FROM THE IN-LAWS, HOLIDAYS, VACATIONS, FANTASY FOOTBALL, THE STOCK MARKET, THE NEIGHBOR'S KID WHO JUST RAN THROUGH YOUR ROSE BUSHES...

It is easy to get distracted, become overwhelmed, and procrastinate.

It has been said before,

"We do not need more time; we need a stronger reason to act so that we use time more effectively."

One thing I force myself to do so I can better utilize my time is

CREATE URGENCY.

I heard a story of a man talking with a woman who complained that she struggled with procrastination.

The man asked the woman, "If I said, 'meet me here tomorrow morning at 4:30 am and I'll give you three million dollars,' what would you do?"

The woman very quickly replied, "I'd be here at 4:15 am," as she smiled and laughed.

The man said, "See, you don't have a procrastination problem, your goals just aren't that important to you. You have no urgency for your goals."

I am sure we would all find a way to wake up super early if three million dollars was on the line. Just look at how early people get up to save $300 on a TV on Black Friday!

You must look at yourself and evaluate the areas of life where you find yourself putting off your goals.

Why aren't you taking the necessary steps toward achieving the goals that you say are important to you?

- Create a sense of urgency to go for your goals.
- Turn "One day, I'll do this" into "I'll do this now."
- Establish deadlines and keep your word to yourself.

#Accountability

When I was getting ready to move to L.A. from Detroit, one of the best pieces of advice I received from an Executive

Producer was, "Pick a day, and no matter what happens, you leave Detroit on that day."

It worked.

I picked my date, February 27th; and when it came, I was in the car, on my way out west.

Picking the day made the goal real. It turned "I want to move to Los Angeles" into "I AM moving to Los Angeles on February 27th."

It created the urgency for me to get things in order, so I was prepared and ready for the move.

Eliminate your 'one day/someday' thinking.

Now is the time to take the first step. Life will continue to happen, and there will always be new obstacles that you had failed to consider.

Life will get in the way.

So, start acting URGENTLY. When you have time today, get it done today.

If you don't trust me, trust **Ben Franklin**:

"Do not put off for tomorrow that which can be done today."

If you don't trust him, trust **Abraham Lincoln**:

"Leave nothing for tomorrow
which can be done today."

It is easier to create urgency when
there is a big enough reward at stake.

If you believed that on the other end of your urgency was three million dollars waiting for you, you'd probably find the motivation and dedication to complete the goal, wouldn't you?

Make sure your goals are big enough to create the urgency in your action to crush the distractions and procrastination.

Be the Urgent Care doctor of your goals!

REASON #17

HOLY SHIT...SHE THINKS SHE'S OLD

"My boss complains about being 'too old.' She thinks that because she didn't get carded when buying alcohol, she's an over-the-hill dinosaur; so then, what does that make me?"

Look, I totally get it. It's annoying to listen to someone talk about 'how bad they have it' when you would love to have their problems. No one wants to hear someone complain about their first wrinkle when your forehead looks like a desert science project.

**"Wow, you have one gray hair.
I spend $150 a month covering all of mine.
Little shit..."**

*Listen, it's all relative.
Remember when you finally made it to high school, and you thought you were so much older and more mature, and you didn't want to have that dino-saur-themed birthday party anymore because you had evolved?*

We all have times we can reflect back on to see how silly or naive we were.

I was the 13-year-old who thought I was so cool and mature, yet I had a comforter on my bed with logos of every National Football League team on it. That's not very "mature," but I would gladly take that thing back. I loved that comforter. (I'd love to see the look on someone's face the first time they walk into my bedroom and find the Detroit Lions draped over my racecar bed.) #VrooomVrooom

We have a tendency to think our problems and insecurities are the most important ones we have ever faced.

Why?

Because it's happening right now — to us — and humans are generally awful at putting things into the right perspective.

Take a second and grab a pen and paper.
(It's okay, I know you aren't going to do this, so I've created some more lines in the book.)

Write down a list of complaints you have about your age.

Ok, limit the complaints to three. Let's not go overboard.

Is your hair thinning? Do your joints hurt when you try to work off that beer belly? Perhaps you're just starting to notice a lack of sufficient energy.
What things are you feeling 'too old' to do? Ok, go!

1.____

2.____

3.____

All set? Did you identify your big three, or are you 'too old and mature' to do what the author of a book asks?

I see you!

Here are some more lines for you. DO THE WORK.

I complain about my:

____

____

____

____

____

Now, here is where it gets fun.

Now that you've written your complaints, ***add 17 years to your current age.***

If you're 35, imagine you are now 52. 48? You're now 65. If you're 56, now imagine you're 73.

HOW DOES THAT FEEL?

Seriously, imagine how you will feel in 17 years.

How much do you think someone 17 years older than you would love to be walking in your shoes?

They might switch with you in a heartbeat.

I am not saying aging is a bad thing; a lot of people have amazing lives in their later years. I can honestly say that I am really excited for my salt-n-pepper hair to start coming in; I think it is going to be a good look for me. **#silverfox**

The reason I recommend this exercise is to show you that it's all about perspective.

Your youthful boss (or co-workers) genuinely believes they are old, simply because they have never been 'older.' It's insecurity at its finest.

Don't get upset with someone else because they have insecurities; all you can do is take control of your own personal insecurities.

Remember, we all have the same 24 hours in a day. Choose to see today as a gift. Stop worrying about the, "OMG, Becky, I am soooo old" comments. Embrace your journey, every beautiful step of the way.

People become trapped by their perspectives, mostly because they don't know any better. They are unfortunately missing out on the opportunity to be thrilled, excited, and grateful for their current age. Do we need to go back to the chapter about gratitude?

Why 17 years, you ask?
Why not? Stop asking questions.
You probably didn't even write anything in the blanks. Moving on...

REASON #18

YOU CAN'T FIRE ME!

"He wants to fire me?
I started this gangster shit.
This is the
Motherfing thanks I get?" ****

Thanks, Ice Cube.

I am going to assume you don't talk like that, and I'm not going to judge you even if you do. I was born and raised in metro-Detroit and loved listening to Eminem, Dr. Dre, Snoop Dogg, Tupac Shakur, and other legendary hip-hop artists.

But this chapter isn't about
hip-hop, it's about you.
And guess what?

You're fired!

Here's a question:
If you were fired tomorrow, what would you do?

? ? ?

Let's do some role-playing.
If your boss called you into their office tomorrow morning and told you they had to let you go, how do you think you would respond?

Would you **cry***?*
Would you **scream***?*
Would you **be calm***?*

Would you think about all the bills you have to pay, or would you think about all the other (better) jobs you could get?

Would you think about how other people would judge you,or would you think about how this turn of events is going to make you stronger?

The truth is, we tend to get comfortable in our situations, and we live in the ILLUSION that change will not happen.

But change DOES happen!

"The only thing constant is change."
– Heraclitus

Whether it is a military battle, a sporting event, a speaking engagement, or a business presentation,

the time to prepare isn't when the obstacle shows up.

You must prepare beforehand.

Develop your game plan, strategy, and emergency survival guide before you have to face the adversity.

Start thinking about getting fired now.

What would be your plan?
Have you set up your finances to handle unemployment?
How can you be proactive instead of reactive?

When you are proactive, you can make proper decisions, so you aren't left feeling like your legs have been swept out from under you.

**Don't let struggles,
hardships,
and failures
cripple your spirit.**

Don't let situational change catch you off guard.
Get out in front of it before it crushes you.

**Be prepared.
Be proactive.
Be ready.**

BE RESILIENT.

When you become resilient, getting fired (or anything else, for that matter) will cease to shock you. When you're resilient, you'll quickly bounce back vs. standing outside, wet, in the cold without any answers.

NOW, if you participated in that little exercise, and getting fired actually sounded like a pretty damn great situation,

IT'S TIME FOR A CHANGE!

Perhaps you're ready to step away but you're unsure about the next step, or you're hoping someone will come along with another opportunity and give you some peace of mind to make the move.

Psst...permission isn't coming.

This is your life, and you do not need anyone's approval to do the things that will make you the happiest and most fulfilled.

Story time!

When I had to go to the bathroom in elementary school, I would raise my hand, the teacher would call on me, and they'd grant me permission.

Then, I could go to the bathroom.

I was required to get approval first to do what I needed to do.

Thank God times have changed!

I no longer ask permission to go to the bathroom. But I did find it necessary to take a look at my life as an adult and identify the areas where I was still **seeking the approval of others**.

Are there areas of your life that have you still waiting for permission to begin?

Are there specific things you are hoping someone will grant you permission to do?

Are you looking for other people to approve of your dreams before you start taking action toward your dreams?

You are an adult.

You do not need to ask for approval to chase your dreams, to make changes in your life, to take steps toward traveling more, to begin that new healthy lifestyle, to write that song...

Many of us were raised to ask permission and rely on other people so much that we forgot how POWERFUL *we really are.*

We grew up looking for a parent or teacher (or boss) to show us the way. But you have the tools and the abilities already within you to get moving toward what you want, and to do the things you need to do.

It's time to get up from that elementary school desk with your hand raised, hoping someone will call on you and give you permission to chase a fulfilling life. Be an independent adult; stand up and take care of business!

"Our deepest fear is not that we are inadequate. Our deepest fear is that we are powerful beyond measure. It is our light, not our darkness that most frightens us."

- excerpt from "Our Greatest Fear"
by Marianne Williamson

REASON #19

SHE HAS THE OWNER'S LAST NAME

"My boss has zero talent, zero skills, zero ambition. Her only qualification is her last name."

Hooray for nepotism!

This one really sucks. The CEO's bumbling son or eccentric daughter can be an absolute energy sucker to the workplace and to your life. Having to deal with someone that is only your boss because they are the close friend or family member of someone important can be a bit demoralizing. You feel like you are busting your ass, you have dedicated yourself to the company, and then someone's personal relationship to your boss overrules all of your hard work and preparation.

I grew up the son of a police officer.

From a young age, I learned how to use my father's occupation to my advantage and would often do my very best to manipulate a situation. There were even incidents where I wasn't even fully conscious that I was using this leverage; those skills were unconsciously learned growing up in my household.

I talked myself out of at least 25 speeding tickets during my high school and college years.
(But not all of them...remember the laundry list of legal problems I mentioned earlier?)

While there are many environments where nepotism creates some major headaches, it is also important to realize that there could be massive benefits that the son or daughter of a person of power brings to the workplace.

Let's look at the boss' kid scenario:

- *It's easy to say, "She hasn't worked hard" or "He didn't earn it."*
- *It's easy to say, "She would be nothing without mommy or daddy."*
- *It's easy to discredit their abilities because you're too wrapped up in your sour feelings.*

Now, let's look at this from another angle:

If a child had been around since the creation of a company and had been coming to work with their parent since they were ten, by the time that child becomes 20, the kid would have ten "peripheral" years of connection to the business. And what's so wrong with building a family business, anyway?

Now, imagine that little kid is you. Score!

With all of your ambitions, hard work, and excitement around learning, if you were involved in your parent's business, you might have five, seven, maybe even ten years' worth of knowledge related to your current position.

The boss' kid had the luxury of getting that training at a younger age, so maybe he has ten years of experience by age 25.

By merely thinking this person started at the top without putting in any work, you may be oversimplifying the situation and undervaluing your boss. More than likely, you're just feeling a bit entitled.

Who's the child, now?

While it is not the same as nepotism, I do want to discuss an equally challenging situation to stomach:

Working for a boss who received the promotion you were up for. Ouch!

This has resentment, bitterness, and comparison written all over it.

The best-case scenario is that it's a person from outside the company, whom you have no preexisting connection or issues with.

Or, you may be in a situation where you are now a subordinate to a boss who was once your peer. Perhaps you were both interviewing for the same promotion, and they received the position instead of you.

It hurts, I know.

Maybe you previously got along, and it won't be such a bad transition. Or perhaps they are the type of person that sends you countless Facebook quizzes and asks you why you haven't replied to them. Either way, it can be a bruise to the ego.

The extreme case:
You have been removed from a position, and now a former subordinate has stepped into your old role. Twist the knife, already!

I'm not going to lie, this can be a difficult pill to swallow.

Simply looking at them may trigger a reminder of what you perceive to be a failure. However, understand that being demoted is not something you should sit around and blame anyone else for.

{When you blame other people, you are giving your power away to them.}

The best qualities that a leader can have are developing the ability to take ownership of your actions and taking responsibility for your mistakes.

If you were demoted, my instinct tells me that there was something wrong. Only you know what it is, but if you can't find *any* fault in yourself, it might be a good time to start searching for potential reasons.

Regardless of where you fall in dealing with in the ol' 'That promotion should have been mine' scenario, there is only one thing to do:

Your absolute best!

There are going to be growing pains anytime there is a change.
Be the person that supports the team.
Be the one who sets the tone of how your department is going to operate.

Show why you are a valuable member of that company.

You're not there to:
show off,
show someone up,
or show the company they made a mistake.

Rather, you're there to be a team player
and to do the job you are being paid to do.

When you showcase the resilience to come back to work and give 100%, even though you didn't get your way, that is the type of character the board of directors is looking for.

There will be other opportunities.

Being a bitter crybaby will not open any doors
but being resilient and hard-working most definitely will.

Plus, you never know when the new boss will get fired or quit themselves.

Be ready; you are on deck, slugger.

Here's a quick note about accepting responsibility and owning your mistakes:

We ALL make mistakes; some are small and trivial; others are massive and embarrassing.

As I mentioned before, in my senior year of high school I was voted "Class Perfectionist." I thought because "perfect" was in the title that it was a compliment! Well done, Phillip!

The word 'perfect' is a trap! Why? Because it doesn't freakin' exist!

When you understand that there's no such thing as perfect, it makes it a lot easier to accept that everyone makes mistakes. It is just part of life.

Don't run from your mistakes. Don't try to spin your mistakes. Don't make a mistake worse by not owning it or by trying to sweep it under the rug or passing the mistake on to someone else.

When you do that, you are just building a house on shaky ground. And, you're trying to protect your ego.

"Control your ego, or your ego will control you."

It's so true.

OWN YOUR MISTAKES.

Admit when you are wrong.

Think back to the last time someone around you admitted they made a mistake.

Did you yell at them even louder?
Did you pile on the guilt?
Or did you respect them for their honesty and try to help them fix the problem?

I bet you handled their admission with care, respect, and trust. The same thing will happen when you admit your own mistakes.

Making mistakes is human, admitting your mistakes is heroic.

Taking responsibility is what leaders do. It's what champions do.

Owning your mistakes is how you build strong character;
It's how you live a life that commands respect.

Hiding from your mistakes only makes you feel smaller in the long run.

Have the courage to admit when you are wrong and do your best to make it right as quickly as possible.

When you take ownership of your mistakes, others will take ownership of theirs by following your example. Finger-pointing and blaming will not produce change nearly as powerfully as OWNING YOUR MISTAKES will.

- **Be courageous, honorable, and humble.**
- **Be honest, truthful, and vulnerable.**

OWN YOUR MISTAKES,
and you will never be a slave to them.

REASON #20

*HE CAN'T GET HIS SH*T TOGETHER*

*"There are just too many things wrong with this guy. He is rude, he is entitled, and he is a crybaby. I hate him. There is no way I can let this sh*t slide."*

I understand that there are people in this world who are difficult to deal with.

They are bullies.
They are self-centered.
They are absolute happiness destroyers.

If that is the type of boss you have, I can only imagine how frustrating that is. I hope you now have the courage, strength, and faith in yourself to get out of that toxic space.

But if the change cannot happen immediately,
in order to save your own sanity, you must:

Forgive your boss for who they are.

Forgiving someone is not the same
as condoning their behavior.

We don't always forgive people for their sake; many times, we forgive others for our OWN emotional freedom.

As we wrap up this book, let's welcome our next week with a spirit of forgiveness that extends beyond the workplace.

Perhaps someone said or did something this past week that upset, hurt, or disappointed you. Maybe it was a friend, parent, spouse, or a child; maybe it was a co-worker or a complete stranger. You might already have someone in mind who you need to forgive.

It has been said,

"Holding a grudge is like drinking poison and expecting the other person to get sick."

We must practice a spirit of forgiveness. We must forgive others so that we can be free.

Forgiving is not being a doormat.
Forgiving isn't devaluing your worth or quality of life.
Forgiving doesn't make you smaller than the other person.

{ Forgiving others brings freedom to ourselves. }

When we forgive, we allow ourselves to unload the burden of negative, toxic thoughts. Forgiveness enables us to put down the emotional weight of judgment.

One of the easiest ways that I find to give forgiveness is to say a kind word about someone.

"That person upset me, but I forgive them, and I hope that their day gets better so they can be better for those around them."

Remember, ***"Hurt* people hurt people."**

If your boss was nasty, rude, or mean, there is likely something going on in their life. It may be considered something small or big to you, but it is big enough to affect how they behave in the world, and you can bet it affects how they feel about themselves. It can be easy to assume that since they are in a position of power, they have their life completely under control; however, your boss is a human who may be taking on a lot of responsibility and is feeling the pressure.

Their external behavior is a reflection of how they feel on the inside.

And while you may have to deal with someone being nasty for some part of your day, they have to live with themselves 24 hours a day. Be kind and offer forgiveness, whether someone "deserves" it or not.

Forgiveness isn't giving them permission to do wrong, it is giving yourself permission to be FREE.

Now, this next little bit of information might feel like it's coming from out of left field, but as a man involved in the substance abuse recovery community, I thought it was important to add. (And it loosely applies to this chapter.)

With the current opioid epidemic in America, as a nation, we are seeing drug addictions and alcoholism skyrocket, and it hits people of all ages, races, and demographics.

People are rampantly self-medicating with drugs, alcohol, and prescription medication to better deal with anxiety, stress, ADHD, PTSD, chronic pain, undiagnosed mental disorders, etc.

While most of us are not doctors, we should keep this in our awareness.

If you are noticing that these types of addictions may be associated with your boss, consider that:

- They could be having a problem at home in their relationship.
- They could be dealing with medical issues of a family member.
- They could be experiencing financial hardships.
- They could be overwhelmed with the responsibilities of being the boss.

Ask your boss how they are doing rather than judging their behaviors. A simple question with the right amount of care, empathetic concern, and genuine curiosity can do wonders.

Have the courage to stand up, show some humanity, and be supportive.

If your boss, co-workers, or workplace environment does become too toxic and it appears there is no escaping the behavior issues running rampant in your office, you owe it to yourself to help make a change.

Among the most common regrets that people have before their death is *"remaining in an unfulfilling career."*

Life is too short to hate your job, your workplace environment, or the people you're working with. Don't get caught living with a bunch of "I wish I would'ves."

Conclusion

"Great...another Millennial just told me how to live my life. I literally can't even."

If you have made it to the end of the book, I hope you enjoyed yourself and took away useful information and a new perspective for your life.

The American workplace is facing many challenges, and ageism is most certainly one of them. Multiple generations with varied backgrounds amongst workers will inevitably bring clashes over ideals and outlooks, and there is a lot of evidence to support that. While we addressed some of these issues, I hope that this book has allowed you to see that there are always opportunities and possibilities in any given situation.

Remember, there were several exercises laid out throughout this book to help you on your journey of life. If you are like most people, you read the book without completing (or even starting) those exercises. Feel free, now that you have finished, to go back and take advantage of those opportunities:

- Integrity Scan .... Page 22
- Updating your thinking .... Page 61
- Projecting Assessment .... Page 104
- Gratitude List .... Page 116
- Age Complaining .... Page 138

Whether someone is a Baby Boomer, Gen Xer, Millennial, or Gen Zer, we all have the ability to go beyond simply coexisting by thriving and learning to grow together.

On the path to self-awareness and self-mastery, we have learned to identify:

Ego * Entitlement * Fear of Failure
Arrogance of Success * Fear of Change

With self-mastery, you must begin with the self.
"Put on your oxygen mask first
before helping someone else with theirs."

When you clean your side of the street, you can powerfully serve other people and create long-lasting happiness and fulfillment for your life and those around you.

REGRET WILL COME TOMORROW
IF YOU DON'T WORK TO DESTROY IT
TODAY!

You have a choice:

Either live your life with purpose, boldness,
courage, acceptance, and resilience,

OR

You may very well one day be lying in a hospital
bed, wishing you had done things differently,
consumed by regret.

DO YOUR FUTURE SELF A FAVOR:

Give yourself a life that you can look back on in your final days, and know you went all out. You lived fully. You overcame fear, you mastered the small feelings, you accepted the challenges, and made the most of your life.

We do not destroy regret in our final moments; we destroy regret TODAY by chasing our dreams, by living a full life, by telling those we love that we love them, and by being bold and courageous.

It has been said that "You only live once, but if you do it right, once is enough." I love that.

I will leave you with this:

"There are plenty of difficult obstacles in your path. Don't allow yourself to become one of them."
- Ralph Marston

Thank you for reading "All the Reasons I Hate My 28-Year-Old Boss."

ABOUT PHILLIP ANDREW BARBB

Phillip Andrew Barbb is a 2x Emmy®-nominated television producer, speaker, and personal development coach based in Los Angeles, California.

Originally from Metro-Detroit, the Michigan State University graduate has dedicated himself to inspiring, encouraging, and guiding people toward living their most exciting and fulfilling lives.

As a Speaker, he travels the country, and through high-energy entertainment and unforgettable storytelling, shares his stories with audiences on a variety of topics including Leadership and Team Building, Peer Pressure and Substance Abuse, and Social Media Influence. He is also active in the Los Angeles County Jail System sharing his experience, strength, and hope with inmates battling drug and alcohol addiction.

As a Personal Development and Executive Coach, Phillip has worked with A-list celebrities, C-suite executives, hosts, authors, experts, and business owners. He works with his clients on emotional intelligence, dynamic leadership, and strategic short-term and long-term goal setting. Additionally, he consults with brand development, improving on-camera speaking techniques, and becoming more effective communicators, both in front of and behind the camera. He advises clients on how to marry their expertise and passion with their vulnerability and authenticity to create lasting positive results in their industries.

As a TV Producer, Phillip is a member of the TV Academy and Producer's Guild of America. As a Producer on the popular psychology show "Mind Field" on YouTube Red, he was honored with two Daytime Emmy® nominations for *Outstanding Education or Informational Series.* He has also worked on programs: "Ultimate Tag" (FOX), "Westside" (Netflix), "Dating #NoFilter" (E! Entertainment), "The Great American Baking Show" (ABC), "Help Us Get Married" (Facebook Watch), "Cults & Extreme Beliefs" (A&E), "Fluffy Food Adventures" with Gabriel Iglesias" (Fuse), "The Briefcase" (CBS), "WWE Total Divas" (E! Entertainment), "Broken Skull Ranch" with Stone Cold Steve Austin" (CMT) and "Undercover Boss" (CBS) for which he holds an Emmy® certificate for his contributions.

Stay current with Phillip Andrew Barbb at www.PhillipAndrew.co, and follow on social media platforms @PhillipAndrewLA.

BOOKS CITED:

- Bungay, M. (2016) *The Coaching Habit*. Toronto, Canada: Box of Crayons Press.
- Burchard, B. (2014) *The Motivation Manifesto.* Carlsbad, CA: Hay House, Inc.
- Chandler, S. and Litvin, R. (2013) *The Prosperous Coach*. Anne Marie, FL: Maurice Bassett.
- Csikszentmihalyi, M. (2008) *Flow: The Psychology of Optimal Experience*. New York, NY: Harper Perennial Modern Classics.
- Gracian, B. (2008) *The Art of Worldly Wisdom.* New York, NY: Barnes & Noble.
- Greitens, E. (2015) *Resilience.* Wilmington, MA: Mariner Books.
- Levine, M. (2009) *The Price of Privilege*. New York, NY: Harper Collins Publishers.
- Pressfield, S. (2015). *Do The Work*. San Bernardino, CA: Black Irish Entertainment LLC.

Made in the USA
San Bernardino, CA
07 January 2020